THE ILLITERATE PROFESSIONAL

THE ILLITERATE PROFESSIONAL

HOW TO BE SUCCESSFUL AND FULFILLED IN YOUR LIFE AND CAREER

TUNDE KUKOYI

The Illiterate Professional

Copyright © Tunde Kukoyi

2020

All Rights Reserved.

Education is the most powerful weapon which you can use to change the world

- Nelson Mandela

Table of Contents

Acknowledgement

I thank my family for their patience and support while I was writing this book. It has been a long journey for us all, as I never knew it would take this long when I started. Thank you to my lovely wife Amanda for being understanding. She was the first person to read this book in its raw form and encouraged me to keep working at it.

I also want to thank my parents and siblings for the lessons and values I learned while growing up in your care. They have remained pivotal in my growth in life all through the years.

Thank you to my friends and colleagues who took the time to read and review my manuscript. Special thanks to Dr Akinpelu Babatunde who has been on this journey with me since the inception of the idea. This book would not have been what it is today without your insights and suggestions. Many thanks to Dr Joseph Kenogbon and Dr Doyinsola Olaniyan for your belief in the quality and potential of the content of this book. I am grateful to my friends at Toastmasters, Shamila Akhtar and Mohammed Kasujee, for your useful and honest reviews and words of encouragement. Many thanks to Miss Folawe Omikunle and the entire Teach For

Nigeria foundation for all the inspiring work they do for the Nigerian children who lack access to good education.

I am thankful to anyone who has selected this book to read. You could have chosen any other book or decided to spend your time in another way, but you decided to give me a chance to pass my message across. I want you to know that this means a whole lot to me.

Most importantly, I am thankful to God for the ability and the insight he has given me to be able to put this piece together. Without him, I could not have done a thing.

Introduction

In the words of the famous American philosopher John Dewey, "Education is not preparation for life; education is life itself." As they appear contradictory, I would never have thought the words 'illiterate' and 'professional' would come side by side in usage but, as you will soon come to understand as you delve into the pages of this book, this is the reality of many. An illiterate is commonly understood as one who cannot read or write, but in the context of this book it describes having little or no education. The word 'Professional' might also seem out of reach to some of you that have picked up this book, but chances are very likely that you are one. Malcolm Gladwell in his book *Outliers* was able to show from research that if you've spent at least 10,000 hours working on a particular sphere of life, you will be better than an average individual in that sphere, and you have earned your right to be called a Professional[1].

We live in a fast-moving world now, and many of the conventional professional jobs are becoming increasingly unpopular among the growing generation. I am also aware that working in conventional 9-5 jobs has received a lot of backlash in recent times. I, however, have a different stance on this subject. I have a lot of praise for the professionals who are keeping our society together. Everyone cannot be an entrepreneur, life coach, or real estate investor. We still need policemen, lawyers, doctors, nurses, engineers, pilots, secretaries, and many others who keep our society together. Without these professionals, I cannot imagine how life would be for most of us. At the time of the writing of this book, the coronavirus pandemic, which started in 2019, is keeping the world on lockdown, and I wonder what the world would have been like if it wasn't for the professionals tagged 'essential workers' - such as the healthcare professionals, law enforcement agents, teachers and supply chain workers who have helped to keep us all alive and sane. I would, therefore, want to make my standpoint clear from the beginning of this book; I respect professionals from every sphere and believe they are integral to our society. However, from my interaction with some of my colleagues, as well as professionals from other fields, I have come to realise too many professionals are frustrated. The popular belief is that this frustration is because they do not love their jobs; but, many times, this is not true. The major reason people are unhappy in their jobs is that they feel they are missing out on life in the process of giving their best to their professions. The intent of this book is therefore not to discourage or degrade professionals, but to show us that there is more to living a successful life than just living within the confines of our jobs or professions. My plan in writing this book is for you to see that you can live a bigger, better and more meaningful life.

As we would all agree, our lives are multi-dimensional, being made up of different aspects: health, relationships, finances, personal growth, career, family, and much more. Although many of us that went to schools and formal training institutions might argue that we are educated, an integral question we need to ask is what sphere or dimension of life this applies to, and how relevant this is going to be to our entire lives. I believe education is not limited to the four walls of schools or institutions, but rather something we pick up right from our childhood days at home, to what we learn in formal schools or trades, and on to what we learn from our everyday lives - such as from books, media and interactions with people.

It is possible to know a lot about one aspect and be a complete novice in the other. In life, some things are '*good-to-knows*' as they do not directly impact our lives, and there are some things that are '*must-knows*' because they have a direct impact on our quality of life and happiness. Self-awareness is in knowing what you know, and what you do not know. It is also knowing about what is going on in your world and not just the world at large. If we are not self-aware, what we will be doing is role-playing, instead of living out our own true lives.

Knowing current world affairs, the most popular musicians, world sport personalities, how to do the latest dance moves on the web, or whatever it is that appeals to you, are examples of the *good-to-knows*. I once chased after the *good-to knows*; I was a member of the quiz club during my time in University, and I was a fan of news channels because they always kept me up-to-date' on what was happening in the world. But these never really paid off. Maybe if I went for knowledge-based quiz shows, like *Who Wants to Be a Millionaire*, this probably would have helped; but what I am almost sure of is that, even if I did win, because I was technically illiterate the short term any gains would have disappeared quite as fast as I got them. We can probably all remember that big uncle or aunt that seemed to know just about everything that was going on in the world, and yet remained unsuccessful. Why was this? The reason is that they probably learnt all the unimportant things in life at the expense of the basic foundational principles.

The *must-knows*, on the other hand, are things like how to handle your family, managing your finances and taking care of your health. The sad thing is that most of the *must-knows* aren't taught in schools or homes today. You have to go out of your way and learn it yourself. Wouldn't it be good to know all the *must-knows* and the *good-to-knows*? Definitely! That would be a win-win scenario. But, as you will find out in this book, we are powerful yet finite beings. Sometimes, you have to sacrifice something for the other. You will sometimes have to unlearn something so you can learn a new thing. When faced with such a decision, I encourage you to go for the *must-knows* over the *good-to-knows,* and your future self will be thankful that you did.

We cannot wholly place the blame on schools or parents for not teaching us all these *must-knows* in due time. The truth is that many of our parents or teachers in schools did not even know many of these things. If they had, they would have taught us, as I know they all truly wanted the best for us. For example, I grew up in a culture where parents trained their children on how to raise morally sound families. In some cultures that I know, the responsibilities of mothers even go as far as teaching daughters how to satisfy their future partners sexually. Trust me, in such an empowering culture, parents would teach their offspring how to live rich and successful lives if they knew the way themselves. Ironically, what many have resorted to instead is to try to force children to study the popular disciplines in universities and secure a job for a living because that is the only answer they seem to have to that question. A friend of mine was once asked to advise a teenager on the choice of a university course. There was a conflict between the teenager and her parents because of the difference of views in which was more likely to lead to success.

When we discussed this issue, we identified that the main thing that brings this conflict across generations is the lack of knowledge of the true ingredients of success. I particularly love the way American anthropologist Margaret Mead put it, "Children should be taught how to think, not what to think." After all, a successful musician is just as good as a successful doctor, or chef, or tradesman, or whatever. We, therefore, concluded that what was more important was teaching the younger ones the principles of success and granting them the freedom to choose their paths towards attaining it. This is one of the main reasons this book was written.

This book is therefore for everyone, young or old, whether you attended some form of school or not, whether you are in a job or not - simply because it addresses some of the *must-knows* in your life, which will ultimately affect all other aspects of your life. I'd like to welcome you on this journey of self-awareness as we explore some concepts I believe everyone must know in life in the quest for success and ultimate fulfilment. Fasten your seatbelts and let us enjoy this ride of self-awareness together.

Chapter 1

The Perfect Example

Talking about many years of formal education, this is where my story starts. I am still in post-graduate medical training, by the way, and still having to read countless books and go through challenging exams - but that's not what this chapter is about. So, let us go back to my story. After my secondary, or high school as some call it, I progressed to university to study Medicine. It was the right thing to do, being one of the top performers in my secondary school and having parents already working in the medical field. Initially, I was offered entry to study Biochemistry instead in the State university, but I took the entry examinations again a year after and eventually got admitted into the dream course: Medicine. My beautiful life had begun in earnest. I, unfortunately, spent a long time in the university system, and it was ten whole years before I graduated as a doctor - mostly because of a broken system which resulted in frequent industrial action by the academic staff of the university. Trust me, it was not because I was a dull student.

As a matter of fact, I finished as the best graduating student in my set - despite the fact I was not the most brilliant student in my class. What I knew I was good at was identifying patterns and predicting outcomes. I was, therefore, able to closely observe the system and identify what was required to excel in exams. At a certain stage during my days in school, I could confidently predict the ingredients for success within the system. As I considered myself smart in this regard, I naturally felt it was going to be easy to translate these ingredients to success in life after school. As many of you will agree, and as I found, life is an entirely different ball game.

Fast forward to a year of post-graduate internship and another of national youth service for graduates in Nigeria. Then I went back to school, again. This time, I undertook a Masters' Program at a prestigious UK university and finished with a Distinction. In total, that added up to 11 years of tertiary education. Assuming I live to be a hundred years old, that will be over ten per cent of my lifetime in getting formally educated (and that is not even primary and secondary education).

I guessed it was finally time to hit the marketplace, and I did. Doctors are in high demand all over the world and I ultimately found myself in the UK marketplace, working and earning one of the highest-rated currencies in the world - the Great British Pound. The life I had always dreamt of had finally begun. I felt, with such a secure job and salary, there was nothing to stop me in living a happy and fulfilled life. Although I consider myself to be relatively sociable and outgoing, I have always kept moderation as my principle. For me, this meant I was not given to things like overly expensive clothes or restaurants, and I never smoked or drank alcohol, even when I was out with friends at clubs and pubs. I never routinely flew in business or first class, or any of that kind of fancy stuff. I naturally expected that, with the combination of a well-paying job and a moderate lifestyle, things were bound to be a smooth sail for me.

As I was already nearing the third decade of my life, I decided it was now time to face life head-on. It was time to get married to the love of my life, and this I did. I spent a decent amount of my earnings on my wedding ceremony, but was still doing fine. However, not long afterwards, a couple of short-term financial setbacks (which included a honeymoon scam, excessive migration costs due to a rejected visa application, being out of work for a couple of months, and having to pay for accommodation in two different countries) brought me to a low point in my finances. I had not planned for all of this and surprisingly began to realise my financial state was beginning to affect my happiness.

I could have easily shrugged it off as one of those things that happen in life and convinced myself that all I had to do was work more and earn more so everything could revert to normal. But I just kept getting this nudge from within telling me there was so much about life that I did not know. It was at this point that I had to take a break and reflect on what a successful life meant to me — was it all about what I had? Should money be so important that it should affect my happiness? If it is, how am I supposed to manage it so that it does not become a source of worry for me? Would my job be sufficient to take care of my family, or would I always have to work for money? How can I be more productive with life? How can I be happy in my job and family? Would I ever have enough to give back? All these questions and more kept spinning in my head and then it dawned on me – I had little or no education outside my professional sphere on many of the things that really mattered in life. I was illiterate.

I took an inward look into my immediate family for answers. My parents, whom I respect so much, have had life going well for them in their professions despite being conservative in their approach. Though I have learned a lot from their values, I yet craved a higher level of impact and reach whilst still operating in the sphere of my professional life. I also looked at my inspiring younger brother who has always been more adventurous and more of a risk-taker than anyone else in my family. Despite being so adventurous, he excelled through school, even up to tertiary and post-graduate education. It was not much of a shock when he decided the entrepreneurial life was the path he wanted to take, despite being professionally trained in Architecture and Urban Design. He was the serial entrepreneur - from poetry and writing, to fashion and cooking, he was always getting himself busy with something. Talking about risk-taking, he also took loans and started businesses which, for a more conservative person like me, was a step too far beyond the boundaries of my comfort zone.

I began to think it was because I took the path of the conventional professional salary/wage earner that I was in my predicament, as I assumed entrepreneurs and risk-takers were more likely to be happy and successful. I, therefore, studied my brother over time to see his outcomes. I realised, despite having so many ideas and breakthroughs, he was just like me in searching for answers to the questions about fulfilment and success in life.

My external search for answers began and, by default, my first step was to go to people in my sphere of influence. I talked to and studied old friends, classmates and colleagues at work - but to my utmost surprise, I was left with more questions than answers. Some of the answers or advice I got were things I either already knew were not going to work, or things that my scientific mind found difficult to accept. It was obvious many of us were not 'enlightened.' I prefer to use the word illiterate for myself because I think it spurs me on, although others might find it rather derogatory.

My search for answers continued, and for me this meant doing something that I would not have expected in my wildest dreams. I had to go back to 'school' to learn the things I missed out early on in life. This time, however, I did not go to a formal institution with four walls and several professors. Instead, I took a journey of self-discovery and education. This time around, I was in charge of what and how I chose to learn, and if I felt something was not a *must-know* for my life, then I was quick to discard it and move on – a luxury which a formal school setting might not have been able to offer.

In the coming pages of this book, I take you on a journey as I share some of the things I have learnt from diverse sources in this quest: books, courses, seminars, networking events and clubs, online teaching videos, and even the experience of others. I am certainly a different person because of these things which I have learned that span across different topics, including personal finance, relationships, time management and health. Although each chapter can stand alone as a short, inspiring write-up, I hope and believe following through with all the chapters will show you the full picture and be an enlightening experience for you - just as writing this was for me.

Chapter 2

Common Sense from a Parable

As a person of Christian faith, I read the Bible and one of the parts I love the most are the parables of Jesus. The fascinating thing about these parables is not only how they apply to spiritual principles, but how they are loaded with a lot of common sense applied to our lives, even in this present age. For example, there is a parable about a man that built his house on sand instead of rocks, which eventually collapsed. This makes a lot of sense in the architectural and engineering world; you have to have a firm foundation before you build, if you want your building to stand the test of time.

However, the parable that I want to refer to in this book is one commonly called the 'parable of the talents.' Though this book is not intended to be a religious book, I would like to share this story or parable in this chapter for those who have never come across it, or as a refresher to those who have. Stay with me till the end of this one, as there is an important lesson to learn from it.

For it will be like a man going on a journey, who called his servants and entrusted to them his property. To one he gave five talents, to another two, to another one, to each according to his ability. Then he went away.

He who had received the five talents went at once and traded with them, and he made five talents more. So also he who had the two talents made two talents more. But he who had received the one talent went and dug in the ground and hid his master's money.

Now after a long time, the master of those servants came and settled accounts with them.

And he who had received the five talents came forward, bringing five talents more, saying, 'Master, you delivered to me five talents; here, I have made five talents more.'

His master said to him, 'Well done, good and faithful servant. You have been faithful over a little; I will set you over much. Enter into the joy of your master.

And he also who had the two talents came forward, saying, 'Master, you delivered to me two talents; here, I have made two talents more.

His master said to him, 'Well done, good and faithful servant. You have been faithful over a little; I will set you over much. Enter into the joy of your master.

He also who had received the one talent came forward, saying, 'Master, I knew you to be a hard man, reaping where you did not sow, and gathering where you scattered no seed, so I was afraid, and I went and hid your talent in the ground. Here, you have what is yours.'

But his master answered him, 'You wicked and slothful servant! You knew that I reap where I have not sown and gather where I scattered no seed? Then you ought to have invested my money with the bankers, and at my coming, I should have received what was my own with interest. So take the talent from him and give it to him who has the ten talents. For to everyone who has will more be given, and he will have an abundance. But from the one who has not, even what he has will be taken away. (Matthew 25:14–29)[2]

While it is possible to interpret this parable in different ways, I would like to draw a practical application from it, because I believe this parable applies to today's world just as it did many years back.

The 'talent' was a designation for a collection of gold or silver, and I read that one talent equated to about twenty years of a labourer's wages. Yes, you read that right - twenty years! So it could be said that the one that got five talents got approximately hundred years of wages, four talents eighty years of wages and one talent twenty years of wages. That was obviously a lot of money.

Many of us might be quick to believe that no one would give us that kind of money. But wait a minute! On average, how many years does an individual work either earning wages or as a self-employed individual before retiring? Probably about forty years, or even more. Well, you might argue, this is not money that was given to me, this is my money. An important question to ask yourself at this point is "Is it really my money?"

The classic book *The Richest Man in Babylon* by George Clason gives us insight on how money that is paid to you in the form of wages, salary or earnings is not solely your money, but largely belongs to services and institutions such as your government, grocery stores, landlord/mortgage company, utility companies, and creditors, etc. who collect this money back from you as and when due. The money that eventually becomes your money is what you pay yourself out of all this, and this is why he encourages us in his book to "pay yourself first."[3]

What lessons on personal finance can we draw from the parable of the talents? Many of us have traditionally been taught that one of the best things to do with our money is to save it. I suppose in ancient times banks rarely, if ever, existed and most people kept their money safe in secret places only they knew about. Today we have the luxury of keeping it safe in banks, either traditional bricks-and-mortar banks or perhaps via online savings. The third servant in this parable was probably just being cautious and decided to 'save' the money by burying it. The other two servants, however, were not satisfied with this approach and decided to trade with what they 'earned.'

I am certain that many of us are currently performing even worse than the third servant in this parable did. I know this because I was once in this class. We do not even save what we have earned, we rather spend it all and wait for the next earnings. Imagine if there was a fourth servant in this parable, who did not even have one talent to give back to the Master. How do you think the Master should have rewarded this servant? I will leave you to answer this question.

The moral implication of this whole story is that we all earn at some points in our lives. The unwise thing to do would be to spend it all and start hoping for more. The not-so-wise thing to do would be to save it and watch inflation catch up to, or even surpass, the money we have saved - thereby reducing its value. The wise thing to do would be to trade with, or invest with, your money. In his book co-authored with Donald Trump *Why We Want You to be Rich*, Robert Kiyosaki said "Money is like talent. It doesn't do much good if you keep it to yourself. It has to be nurtured. It has to be used properly. It takes time, work and patience."[4]

I would like to propose, as illustrated in the parable, that money is talent. And just as we have seen, those who merely save alone or spend all they earn would have the little or nothing they have left taken away from them, whereas those who trade and invest with their resources would have more flowing towards them. That is what differentiates the rich and the successful from the poor and miserable today.

Learning from Practical Examples

Meet Grace Groner (1909-2010)

Grace Elizabeth Groner was born in 1909 in Lake County, Illinois. She and her twin sister Gladys were orphaned at the age of 12 and were helped by a prominent member of their farming community named George Anderson. The Anderson family loved Grace and Gladys and helped pay the fees for boarding school and tuition at Lake Forest College, from which they graduated in 1931.[5]

Following graduation, Grace went on to work as a secretary for Abbott Laboratories, where she worked for about four decades. Although Grace was known to travel widely, she lived a modest life as she never got married or had kids, and lived in only one house. She loved to walk everywhere she went and so never needed a car.

In 1935 at the age of 25, whilst still working as a secretary, Grace invested some of her income by purchasing three shares of Abbott Laboratories stock valued at $60 each, making a total of $180. Her investment turned out to be a profitable venture as the company reportedly increased its dividend pay-out for 50 years in a row. As Grace's shares continued to split and her dividends continued to increase, she kept reinvesting the dividends each time.

Although Grace did not inherit any wealth, she was able to give back from what she earned for decades, without having to scrimp and save. She was reported to have donated anonymously on several occasions and even volunteered as a secretary at the First Presbyterian Church and Barat College in her later life. She remained passionate about education, always remembering the gift of education offered to her by the Andersons in her early life. She, therefore, remained close to Lake Forest College, always attended football games and even donated $180,000 to start a Scholarship Fund.

Grace Groner was, therefore, a humble lady who most would have thought lived a pretty ordinary life. Her long-time friend and attorney William Marlatt said about her: "She enjoyed other people and every friend she had was a friend for who she was, not what she had." Grace's story, however, surprised the whole world when she left behind a huge sum of $7.2 million to Lake Forest College through a foundation she had established just before passing away at the age of 100, all from the investment which started from $180 in stocks. It was so surprising that the college president at the time, Stephen Schutt, nearly fell off his chair when he heard this and exclaimed, "Oh, my God!" Today, Grace Groner's legacy lives on through her foundation and it is estimated that 1,300 students will benefit from her will.[6]

Reflecting on lessons we have drawn from the parable of the talents, it can be said that Grace, who started with an investment of $180, ended up with $7.2 million when the Master returned. Simple saving cannot achieve such a feat. Lavish spending would not even get you close. The way Grace achieved this was through patient and diligent investing, while allowing the natural force of compounding to take its effect. Grace truly personifies the common sense that this parable of the talents teaches us — trade with, and invest, your earnings or they will be taken away from you.

Reflection and Action Steps

- Take some time to calculate your estimated total earnings since you started earning in life. Note this doesn't have to be absolutely accurate. This is just a number for reflection.

- Take some time to add up the estimated value of all your possessions.

- Compare these two estimates. Are you holding on to your 'talent', reducing its value or increasing it?

- Calculate your current monthly earnings. How much of this are you retaining?

- What are you doing with the money you are saving up from your earnings? Are there better things you can do with the money?

- Making a list of these would be a good place to start.

- Automate your savings and investments deductions from your salaries or earnings, so that they are deducted before you think about spending them. This is how to pay yourself first.

Chapter 3
The Greatest Investment

What would be the greatest thing to put your money into today, rather than saving it up somewhere or squandering all of it? Could it be real estate and property, or a business or stocks or commodities, such as gold or diamonds, or cryptocurrency? Many of these means of investing have been proven to yield good returns, but they are not comparable to investing in yourself. Yes, you read that right - your greatest possible investment is investing in yourself.

How then do you invest in yourself? You invest in yourself by channelling your resources towards the development of your skills and literacy. Too many people underestimate the potential of this. For example, you can improve your public speaking skills so much that you are paid a hundred times more than what you would possibly get now to do the same thing. Returns on investing in yourself can be as good as infinite.

We may fairly argue that we have already invested in ourselves by paying our way through college or university. But, as I asked earlier, how much of what you learnt applies to the way you live your life right now? The moment when you realise you are ready to invest in yourself is when you are prepared to give up just as much time and/or money than you have spent on your entire formal education to invest in your self-development and improve your 'saleability.' This could be paying for mentorships, seminars, coaching or specialized courses that improve your knowledge in a specialized field, and that will increase your income-generating capability.

The truth is that many of the rich and successful people we know today, who sometimes claim to be 'self-made,' have paid for this self-investment one way or the other in the past. This might have been through paid or unpaid mentorships, learning from their rich parents or even going through specialized training in their field of business. You will agree with me that many of these things sometimes take sacrifices, and resources like money, time, or even the opportunity cost of doing something more popular instead. This is why I smile inside when some people are quick to say that rich people don't want to teach other people how to become rich. Many times, it is because these successful people had to give up something really important to learn it, and would probably not just give it away to someone who won't appreciate the value of such information. It is a well-known fact that people who don't pay do not pay attention.

Another sure way you can invest in yourself is by reading books and watching videos that can improve how you live your life. If you ask successful people in the world their secret to getting wealthy, you will find a common denominator among most of them is that they read books. You will find this habit started when most of them had virtually nothing, continued through their wealth-making process and remains an important part of their daily schedules today. Have you ever wondered why these people, who sometimes run multiple companies and organisations at the same time and have sometimes been known to cut off ties with friends and families due to their commitments to their business or craft, still hold dearly to their habit of reading books? Reading opens your mind to a lot of information that gets your brain working and able to process thoughts better. It also allows you to learn from some of the greatest minds in the world that you ordinarily might not have physical contact with. It helps you to get answers to the questions you have always itched to ask these people, and shows you the methods they used to get to where they are today. Besides, the habit of reading helps to improve your focus; a trait that can be transferred to other important tasks in life with good results.

A common question people ask is which genre of books or what format of books to read. This is a question that I recommend you answer for yourself, because you know what you want from life and also what works for you. Truth be told, the mere act of reading any type of book will improve your life in ways such as I have described above; but the problem is there is only so much time and there are so many books in the world. If you are looking to improve your habits and attitude, I would personally recommend self-help books or autobiographies; if you want to improve your spiritual life, there are books in that field as well. There are books on family, finances, health and many more besides. While I do not recommend reading a lot of fiction, I understand they can help to improve your vocabulary and writing skills. They can also be good relaxation tools, but I would advise you to be mindful of the time you spend on them.

An entrepreneur named Daniel Ally has been credited for this saying: "If you want to know a poor man, look at the size of his television. And if you want to know a successful man, look at the size of his library." While the television and library can be taken as metaphors, as it is possible to learn from entertainment devices such as your phones, computers or television in today's age, the message remains clear – successful people invest in their self-development, while poor people invest in their pleasure and entertainment. My closing advice to you in this chapter is to get enlightened. That you have read this book this far is a good sign that you can do it!

Learning from Practical Examples

Meet Bill Gates (1955-)

William Henry Gates III (Bill Gates) was born and raised in Seattle, Washington in 1955. His father is a retired Seattle attorney and his late mom was a schoolteacher. He is an American business magnate, philanthropist and investor. He is best known as the co-founder of Microsoft, although he has stepped down from the roles of Chairman and CEO of this organisation. He currently chairs and runs the Bill & Melinda Gates Foundation. He is regarded as one of the most successful entrepreneurs, if not *the* most, of the 20th century.[7] He has occupied the Forbes 'Richest Man in the World' spot more times than any other person in the last 25 years.

Bill has been a voracious reader from a young age, as his parents encouraged him to read.[8] He attended Lakeside School and went to Harvard University briefly before dropping out to work on his Microsoft business in conjunction with his partner Paul Allen. Today, he still reads about 50 books a year (an average of about one book per week) despite his many commitments. For him, reading is more than just a pastime; he has described it as essential for his success. He admits that reading helped fuel his curiosity about the world, which was a major driving force in both his career at Microsoft and in the work of his foundation.

Bill's learning and self-investment don't end with reading books alone. He is also known to have a close relationship with billionaire investor Warren Buffett, whom he has referred to on several occasions as his mentor. Bill admits his business education began the day he met Warren on July 5, 1991. In one of his articles for the Harvard Business Review, Bill wrote: "There's nothing I like so much as learning, and I had never met anyone who thought about business in such a clear way."9 Today, Bill has over 60% of his wealth invested in stocks through his foundation. The philosophy behind this is to use capital from the investment to support businesses to provide solutions to complex and entrenched problems in society.[10]

Bill Gates also credits Buffett for teaching him how to deal with tough situations and think long term. He admits that Warren taught him that the measure of his success was not based on his net worth, but on caring about people and them loving you in return. The lessons he learnt from Warren reflect in how he and his wife run the Bill & Melinda Gates Foundation, founded in 2000, through which they have given over $28 billion. Bill Gates and Warren Buffett also started 'The Giving Pledge,' which is an invitation to the billionaires of this world to publicly commit to giving the majority of their wealth to philanthropy.

Bill Gates has demonstrated that investing in himself has not only helped him become one of the richest men in the world, but also that ongoing self-investment through mentorship has helped him stay rich, as well as find personal fulfilment.

Reflection and Action Steps

- When was the last time you picked up a personal growth book or attended a course or seminar?

- Write down one skill which you would like to improve in the next year.

- Search for videos online that teach this skill for beginners.

- Search online for a book or course that addresses that skill.

- Take out of some of your money to pay for that book or course.

- How do you feel after you paid for this? Do you feel like you are beginning to take charge of your life?

Chapter 4

The Twin Siblings

I am going to be a little selfish here and use a medical illustration to explain this concept. Imagine you know a set of identical twins; you would expect them to look alike and grow at the same pace. However, this is not always the case. For example, if they live under different conditions where one is well-fed and the other is starved, then they may not turn out to be the same size after all. Also, if one of them has a debilitating condition such as cancer, that twin is likely to be emaciated compared to the other.

In your financial world, there is a set of twins as well - named Income and Expenses. Many of us professionals fail to recognise that they are identical. We believe that the solution to our problems is more and more of Income to take care of our Expenses, which is true at face value. But if we all know the answer to one of the greatest problems facing man, why then do most people still find this a hard nut to crack?

It might be helpful to know that these twins never had a fair share from the start. Expenses has an eating disorder called Liability that always makes it hungry, and therefore tends to grow bigger with time. Income, on the other hand, has a debilitating illness known as Tax that always makes it smaller than it should be. So, the natural tendency is for Income to stay smaller than it should be, and Expenses keeps growing bigger than it should be.

Therefore, the answer to the big question we always ask is to INTENTIONALLY FEED YOUR INCOME AND STARVE YOUR EXPENSES. I am sure this is a saying most of us are already familiar with. What I realised recently was that, although most of us are familiar with this saying, we do not know how to achieve it. Remember the *must-knows* in life? This is one of the *must-knows*. You must know how to increase your income and reduce your expenses. Everyone who has become, and stayed, rich knows and practises this - at least to an extent.

It is wise not to ignore one of them, while focusing on the other. We are all familiar with at least one sportsperson, movie star or music artist who through hardwork, talent, genius or a stroke of luck became extremely (and sometimes unbelievably) rich and then dead-broke a few years down the line. Many of them never saw this coming. The simple reason is that while their Income was at its biggest state, their Expenses naturally grew to meet the level of their Income - which is not an entirely bad thing, as I have shown that it is only natural. Their mistake, however, was in failing to intentionally feed their Income whilst starving their Expenses. Rather, they encouraged the eating disorder in their Expenses by purchasing more Liabilities, hence their Expenses became insatiable and literally ate their bank accounts to ruin and bankruptcy.

The aim of this chapter is not to spell doom, but rather to enlighten us on how to feed our income as well as starve our expenses. As you must have realised at this point, this book is not one of those books that are intended to unravel hidden secrets, but to highlight the things you have always known but never really paid sufficient attention to. I would, therefore, present another well-known fact to you at this point; the way to feed your income is through creating alternative or passive sources of income, upgrading your skills and the acquisition of assets.

I remember having a debate with my wife recently on whether we can regard ourselves as assets. Technically, the answer is both Yes and No. You can refer to yourself as an asset since your work, trade or use of your talents yields income. Also, remember earlier in this book I highlighted the greatest investment is in yourself. So realistically, YOU, including your skills and capabilities, should be listed as one of your key assets. The problem with relying solely on yourself as an asset is in the natural limitations that hold every human being.

Most people are paid based on the number of hours they work, and we all know that it is virtually impossible to work all day, all year round. Even if it was possible, there are times when you cannot work because of other commitments like family, interests, and holidays, etc. There is also the limitation of old age and/or ill-health, one of which will eventually catch up with every human being. So, if humans as assets are limited, it makes sense to invest in material and potentially limitless ventures. Warren Buffet, one of the greatest investors of all time, was credited with the saying:

"If you don't find ways to make money while you sleep, you will end up working for money till the day you die."

It is therefore imperative that all of us invest in ourselves, our skills and knowledge that will enable us to know the right channels to put our resources into - so that they can keep making money for us, even when we are not working. There are so many misconceptions about assets nowadays, especially through the influence of social media. We are made to believe that your net worth is a product of the assets you have, which should include things like multiple houses, cars, private jets, expensive clothing, etc. This is completely untrue. Many people have these things and their net worth is in negative figures. Simply put, your net worth is the difference between your assets and your liabilities. Robert Kiyosaki's illustration in *Rich Dad, Poor Dad* represents one of the simplest but the most relevant explanation of these concepts. An asset is anything that continually brings in money into your pocket (thereby increasing your income) and a liability is anything that continually takes money out of your pocket (thereby increasing your expenses).[11]

So back to today's misconception about assets. When you want to classify the things you own, you should ask yourself if this object is bringing money into my pocket or taking money out of my pocket. Do not get me wrong; most of us aspire to buy our cars, live in our own houses, and wear good clothes - all of which is completely reasonable. I would never advise you not to get these good things in life. The truly rich people also have these things as well, but for them, unlike most of us, they also serve as assets. Their multiple houses are constantly bringing in rent, their cars and jets are used for private lease, and they are even paid to advertise the clothes they wear. Try to remember this whenever you try to live like the celebrity next door!

While I am not encouraging you to live a miserable zero-expense life, the important message which I am trying to pass across, and which shouldn't be missed, is that these expenses should only be second place to acquiring assets first. This is one of the major differences between rich people and the average-to-poor. Rich people acquire assets first and buy liabilities with the income these assets bring, while poor people buy liabilities and have nothing left to acquire assets. That you cannot eat your cake and have it is an odd-sounding but true principle in life. But remember that some people can have their cakes first and then eat from it without really diminishing the cake.

Feeding Your Income

Many of us have been stuck in a job or at a wage level for several years, and we must be wondering how we can selectively feed our incomes to grow larger than they are at present. The truth is feeding your income is more difficult than starving your expenses, but it is still possible. Our present incomes are just a reflection of the value we provide to the marketplace, and also dependent on the level of our skills and how easy it is to replace us.

I believe in the dignity of every job. But if I asked you, for example, would it be easier to release a cleaner or a CEO from an organisation in the event of downsizing, you would agree with me that it would be the cleaner. Finding a replacement for the CEO would be a more difficult task as certain criteria would need to be met, and such individuals are scarce in the world. It is, therefore, no surprise that the CEO has a higher income than the cleaner. Let us now assume the cleaner decides to develop more skills and becomes an expert at things like interior decoration, decontamination and pest control, garment laundering and care; you will agree such a cleaner has just made himself or herself more valuable, and therefore more irreplaceable, and is therefore worthy of a higher income. The point I am trying to bring out from this illustration is encourage you to make yourself more valuable in whatever skill or profession you practise, and naturally your income will increase. If your income does not, in fact, increase, you are entitled either to demand it from your employers or leave for somewhere were your skills will be better appreciated and remunerated. A typical example can be drawn from the field of medicine where I work. The more specialised you are, the more valuable and irreplaceable you are, and ultimately the more income you earn.

Another way of feeding your income is to open alternative sources of income. This might be a more convenient option if it is not possible or desirable to improve your skills. These alternative sources of income have traditionally been referred to as 'passive.' Many people have been misled by this term, as to some it denotes you do not have to do any work to get it started - but this is completely untrue. The term 'passive' in many instances means that your initial hard work for a period begins to yield continuous rewards, even when you become hands-off. There are many possible avenues for passive income, such as multilevel and affiliate marketing, franchises, infopreneurship, self-serving machines or businesses, space rentals, public speaking and many others. If you look closely at any of these, you will agree that you have to do your initial bit of work to get it going, and thereafter you can sit back and reap the rewards.

Let us take a look at multilevel marketing, for example. Many people have wrong misconceptions about this, thinking it's either too good to be true or it's for lazy people who want to make money without working. The truth, however, is that it works - and it isn't for the lazy. The work is in getting leads and referrals, and getting commissions and rewards for them as you help the provider company to increase their sales. How about infopreneurship (also known as the 'knowledge industry')? Can you just create books, podcasts or videos in a few minutes that will be of value to the world, without any research or reflection? The answer is that it's very unlikely. You will need to take some time to do your research, soul-searching, brainstorming, editing and marketing before you can yield the rewards from people purchasing or subscribing to your product. To summarise on this passive income matter, I would say you can certainly enjoy the fruits of passive income, but you need to take time to plant the seed and nurture the tree before this can be a reality.

Starving your Expenses

The extent to which you can starve your expenses is just as impactful as how you feed your income. Like I said earlier, for many people this might be the easier one to start with because you can start here and now, and notice immediate results. The key behind being successful at this approach is intentionality; if you leave your expenses unchecked, they will always grow to meet up with your income, regardless of how much you are making, and may even surpass your income.

So how can we selectively starve our expenses? For most people living in developed societies, the largest expense is tax. An average middle-class worker in many developed countries pays as much as 40%-50% of their earnings as tax. That is mind-blowing. What is even worse is that you even get taxed on any extra money you make from what is left over, whether this is interest tax, capital gains tax or inheritance tax. This is not to make a case against taxation because, having lived in different economic climes in the world, I can attest that governments with proper taxation systems (coupled with judicious use of these funds) provide the best standards of living for their citizens. My point on starving your expenses with relation to taxation is that you absolutely must pay your taxes, but you should not pay more than you are legally required to pay. This brings to light the very different concepts of 'tax avoidance' and 'tax evasion.'

Tax avoidance is when you minimize your taxes within the confines of the legal system, while tax evasion is when you do not pay your legally required taxes. If our taxes are the biggest expense most of us as professionals have, then why should we not understand what is taken from us, and why it is being taken? I am amazed when I find professionals, such as some of my colleagues, who do not understand their tax bill and how it is being calculated. You need to know where your money is going. If you can spend over 10,000 hours working in whatever field of life you are, surely you should be able to spend a few hours to learn and understand this? Another reason you need to learn how tax works is that there are certain tax advantages in every country that you can benefit from.

For example, there are tax-advantaged accounts such as individual savings or retirement accounts, tax refunds on costs spent on your employment, and so on. This is what many rich people and business-owners have learnt and can take advantage of. If you need further advice on this, you can speak to a certified financial adviser, or even call up the taxation agencies in your country and they will be sure to give you advice tailored to your circumstances. Some of the other expenses we encounter have to do with our lifestyle. Major things would include rent or mortgage payments, car payments and insurance, utility bills, food, clothing and other subscriptions. The key step in getting your act together with regards to these expenses is to assess how much goes to what and where can you make major changes, or even minor tweaks, that would save you some money.

With regards to rent or mortgage payments, could it be downsizing your house, refinancing your mortgage at a lower interest rate, moving into cheaper accommodation, or changing to a less expensive city? As for your car payments and insurance, could it be changing to a less expensive (yet reliable) car, moving closer to work so you do not need a car, or shopping around and negotiating better deals with insurance providers? For utility bills, is there any way you can reduce your consumption, or switch to more efficient and cheaper suppliers? Are you eating out a lot rather than cooking at home, or buying branded products when supermarket brands of the same quality cost way less? Are you recurrently subscribing for things you do not use, such as over a hundred channels of TV, holiday packages that are not saving you any money, or magazines that you never get to read?

The whole essence of this section is to get you to sit down with your credit card and bank statements and have a good look through to discover how you can make meaningful savings by cutting out or reducing things that you don't need, or can do without. The aim of this is not to live a miserable life, but rather to have enough left over to invest and make meaningful and lasting change to your life. Remember it is not about what you earn, but about what you keep.

Lastly in this section, I want to talk about debts as these can be a major source of outgoings for many of us. Traditionally, we are made to believe having a pile-load of debts shows that you are not financially responsible and should, therefore, be avoided. Just as everything in this world is not black and white, having debt does not necessarily denote a bad thing. Just as there are people who have gone bankrupt through debt, there have also been people who have become extremely wealthy because they took on some debt at some point in their lives. The key is what this debt is incurred for and, more importantly, how it is managed - regardless of what it was intended for. This discussion is linked with the concept of assets and liabilities. Most of us take on debts for liabilities, and therefore we have further pressure when it comes to paying off the debts - we not only have repayments to make, but also must cover the interest cost. Robert Kiyosaki in his book *Rich Dad, Poor Dad* refers to these kind of debts as 'bad debts.' 'Good debts', on the other hand, are those that are taken on to invest or to purchase assets that will pay back the debts and provide ongoing income thereafter.[11] You must have a clear plan for the use of these funds and the payback before taking on such debts, as good intentions can go sour if not carefully thought through.

In the next chapter in this book, I will show you some ways to acquire assets and increase your investments - but remember the list is not exhaustive. Find what works for you (I mean literally working for you, even when you are asleep) and stick to it.

Learning from Practical Examples

Meet Shaquille O'Neal (1972-)

Shaquille Rashaun "Shaq" O'Neal was born in Newark, New Jersey in 1972. He is best known as one of the greatest NBA basketballers of all time, with a career spanning 19 years. Naturally, as a famous sportsperson, he earned a lot of money during his sports career. Shaq is, however, not your average basketballer; not just because he is 2.16m tall and weighs 147kg, making him one of the tallest and heaviest players ever, but because of the sound financial moves he has been able to accomplish since he retired from the game in 2011. He was reported to save and invest up to 75% of his income at the peak of his career. Unlike most professional athletes that struggle with their finances post-retirement, Shaq has been able to quadruple his net worth after retirement.

Although Shaq has never left the media spotlight since he retired, as he still hosts his reality shows and holds roles such as a sports commentator, he is not very fond of flaunting his investments. As you would expect, someone with a massive income as his in his prime years as a basketballer would have been a likely target for fraudsters - and Shaq admits he didn't always get it right with his investments, especially in his early years. He fell for a couple of get-rich-quick schemes that promised unimaginable returns in a very short time. However, when he worked on his investment knowledge he changed his strategy similar to one used by Amazon founder Jeff Bezos; he focused on investments not primarily because of the money involved, but rather based on products he loved and believed in their ability to change people's lives. He began to yield good returns.[12]

Some of the ventures Shaq has invested in include, but are not limited to, the following: he owns over 155 franchises of the popular Five Guys, thereby owning up to 10% of their portfolio; he also invests heavily in Auntie Anne's, which is part of the Krispy Kreme chain. Shaq also invests heavily in sports, personally owning forty 24-hour fitness locations/gyms. Mr O'Neal has also invested and made a fortune from investment in technology, most notably his investments in Google in 1999 before the company became public; and he also holds stakes in Apple. Shaq is not left out of the real estate sector; he has stakes in several residential and commercial properties, and also owns several nightclubs in Vegas. In the auto industry, Shaq personally owns 150 carwashes, and also has an endorsement with the General Auto Insurance company.[13]

There is no telling what Shaq is going to invest in next. With all these investments, he has been able to amass a net worth of about $400 million. Shaq has therefore reliably demonstrated how feeding your income through the acquisition of assets and worthy investments, while starving your expenses, can be the ultimate game-changer in your wealth journey.

Reflection and Action Steps

- Calculate your average monthly income from regular earnings and any additional source(s).

- Calculate your average monthly expenses, including fixed and variable expenses. A look at your previous months' bank statements would be helpful.

- What is the difference between your income and your expenses? Is it a positive or negative figure, or is it just zero? There is always room for improvement.

- How do you feel about increasing the margin between your income and your expenses?

- What can you do to increase your monthly income? Can you increase your earnings from your primary employment by increasing your skillset or additional certification? Would you rather consider getting an additional source of income?

- Run through a list of your possessions. How many of them are assets that bring extra money to you? Have you thought of any asset you can add to your possessions?

- What can you do to reduce your monthly expenses? What one thing can you cut off from your life now that would save you some money?

- How many of your possessions are liabilities - constantly taking away money from you? Is there any of them that you can get rid of?

- Do you understand the tax system in your country? Are you taking advantage of the tax benefits? If not, is there someone who can explain it to you?

- Do you have any debts currently? Are they good debts or bad debts? How are you planning to pay them off?

Chapter 5

Are You Working for Money?

'I work for my money!' This is a popular statement from us professionals and, truthfully, we work hard, earn and deserve our money. Hard work pays off and should be instilled in everyone who intends to succeed. This leads us to commend and justify ourselves when we work so hard and make enough money to become comfortable. Being comfortable, however, is not the true definition of success. I have seen far too many professionals fall into this trap. What makes this obvious is when, for some reason, the professional is unable to work anymore because of old age, sickness, redundancy, economic crises, etc. These things do happen and can turn around a previously comfortable household to one that is struggling just to get by.

So, should we work harder and longer now that we can save up more for the rainy days? This seems plausible, but it might be a faulty way of reasoning. If working harder and longer is the only way to earn extra income, you need to take a break and think about this. How many more active and productive hours have you got left in you? Would you spend these all working for money, or would you rather have money working for you? Would you forever be an employee for money or have money be your employee? The choice is yours. You should aim to trade money for your time, not your time for money. Remember the saying of Warren Buffett once again: 'If you don't find a way to make money while you sleep, you will work until you die.'

Money works, too. What is even better is that money can be your slave and keep producing more 'money offspring' that also automatically have to keep working for you, unless you decide to set them free.

Most successful people have learnt this truth and have therefore incorporated working smart into their hard work. They have found the ways that money can work for them, even while they sleep or are on holidays, or at times when they are just not fit to work. There are many innovative ways of making money reproduce itself, with newer ones springing up each day with technological advancement. However, there are some time-tested and proven ones and we will touch upon a few of these in this chapter.

The Stock Market

I have always dreaded the stock market. I am sure I am not alone in this. A lot of you reading this have never, and would never, consider investing in it. Many of us think it is just a game of luck, where the odds are already stacked up against you. A lot of the fear we get about the stock market mainly stems from the fact that we already feel so powerless due to our lack of understanding about how it works. To make things even more difficult, we are bamboozled with all the complexities financial analysts throw at us. Try watching money news channels and you wonder how all the analysis of all the world markets are relevant to how much money we have in our bank accounts. Adding to this would be the story of 'someone we know' who lost a fortune from the stock market. We always know that one person. Need I say more? Probably not. When it comes to the stock market, we just shut our ears and turn to the other side and scream, "Leave me alone!"

I am sorry to burst your bubble, but the stock market is one of the most tested and surest ways of accumulating wealth in the world we live in today. The stock market has yielded an average return of about 10% per annum over the past 100 years.[14] This is not to say that there aren't yearly fluctuations, periods of bear markets (downturns of over 20%) or even all-out recessions, but none of these last forever - because as long as there are still producers and consumers in this world, businesses will continue to find their feet and thrive. For this reason, for a patient investor who is in for the long haul, the stock market is guaranteed to yield good returns.

I have therefore brought you some good news. Investing in the stock market is not as complicated as people on the inside make it seem, and what is more interesting is that there are many ways of investing in the stock market today without being a guru at it. This is not to say that you should invest in something you know nothing about, because that would be extremely risky and could go bottoms-up. Simply put, I believe one of the best ways of making money in the world is lending money and getting it back with interest. This is basically what most banks do. They promise those who 'save' their money a little interest on their bank deposit and give this same money out as loans to individuals and companies at a higher rate. In the same vein, the stock market is based on the principle of lending money. You are, effectively, lending companies and firms money, with the assurance that if the company does well in the financial year, you get your share of the profit.

Also, as the company grows in net worth, so also does the value of your shares; and in the event you decide to sell them, you have a win-win scenario. However, this only applies if your shares are appreciating in value. If your shares are depreciating, you are ultimately losing money. The big question, therefore, is how do you identify the fool-proof ventures to invest in? The truth of the matter is that most people, including financial advisers, cannot tell you for certain how each stock will do. Helpful places to start, however, would include brands that you personally use, believe in their potential to grow and have a proven track record. If you cannot pick any of these, then it is worth considering index funds or exchange-traded funds that track the best performing sectors in the whole market, with low maintenance fees. This is what I do and would also recommend for other professionals who would potentially like to invest in the stock market with a relative 'hands-off' approach. Obviously, everyone's risk tolerance varies but, generally speaking, the younger you are, the more allowance you should have for a higher risk approach. The older you are, and the closer you are to retirement, the more you should start balancing your portfolio with lower-yielding, but more secure, investments such as bonds.

Just start somewhere and keep investing at regular intervals; over time these purchases will coincide with the high points and low points of the market, a technique called cost-averaging. Then leave the rest of the recipe to time and compounding, and you will be amazed at what returns you will get many years down the line.

Real Estate and Properties

This is another wealth-building strategy that has existed for many years, and will continue to thrive for those who are knowledgeable in this field for as long as we continue to live on earth. My prediction is that if humans eventually decide to relocate to Mars, the business would become even more lucrative, as it would be a 'first to grab' opportunity. In their book *Get Rich, Stay Rich and Pass it On*, Catherine McBreen and George Walper were able to show (based on more than ten years of research) that America's wealthiest families, regardless of their backgrounds, have almost 70% of their investment assets in real estate.[15] To put this straight, investing in real estate is not a secret of the rich and successful, it is commonplace knowledge. So why are people reluctant, and why do some people fail at it?

To the outsider, investing in real estate is simply buying land or properties, and then selling or renting to those who need it. Any dummy can do that, right? But contrary to popular opinion, the real estate world is vast and can be complex to the outsider. It ranges from less complicated ventures such as rent-to-rent and serviced accommodations, buy-to-lets, houses of multiple occupancies or even social housing schemes, to more complicated projects such as commercial buildings, office developments and land developments. Even the hotel chains, and some fast-food chains, are investing in real estate and properties. The most beautiful thing about real estate is that you don't necessarily have to own a property to make money; you can just be an information provider, such as an estate or lettings agencies - or possibly just source well-packaged real estate deals to other potential investors for a commission.

Another way you can invest in real estate without actually owning property is through what is known as Real Estate Investment Trusts (REITs). Just like shares, investing in REITs means you are lending the company money to buy prime commercial properties, and you are therefore paid dividends regularly. Also, the value of your investment increases with the value of the property, and you can decide to sell quickly and easily without selling actual real estate property. None of these ventures is technically better than the other, as you can virtually make a fortune from any of these. What is important is to understand which of these is most appropriate for you in terms of your capital, time and experience.

As easy and straightforward as all these ventures might seem, each one comes with its legal frameworks and technicalities, as well as pitfalls to avoid. If you ask thousands of smart people who have lost money in real estate why this happened, most of them would tell you (if they were honest) it was because they didn't know about, or research well enough, what they invested in. This serves as a reminder of what I said earlier about investing in yourself. There are tips and tricks for every trade. You sometimes need to learn under someone who has vast experience in this field, or go on seminars and courses that will teach you how to operate in that area. Very few people would cringe if I asked them if they would pay a huge amount to get a sleek new car or gadget, but if I asked them if they would pay the same amount to learn a new skill such as public speaking or negotiating sales, I'd be sure to get loads of responses like, "Hell, no!" If you are in this category, I would kindly ask you to flip back to the chapter on The Greatest Investment and internalise it.

Business and Sales

Is there a need in your environment that you have identified? Is there something you think you can sell? Is there a service you think you can provide that people would be willing to pay for? There is a potential business in virtually every work or phase of life. The key is identifying this and being ready to sit tight and give it what it takes. I like to think of it this way: humans have needs. The most basic of these include food, clothing and shelter. The unique thing about these basic needs is that even when finances are extremely tight, you still have to take care of them - so there is always business in these fields. The needs of humans are, however, evolving and are not limited to these basic needs alone. Other needs in today's world include the need for convenience, comfort, belonging, security, information, communication, and luxury, amongst others. If you can find a way to provide for these needs, you have found a potential business channel through which you can make yourself some money.

Although starting a business is easy, it is important to note that it is not for the faint-hearted. This is a reason why many people never go into business. As with many things in life, there will always be ups and downs in business, and it takes some strong will and resilience to stay in the game. A core reason why many businesses fail is that the owner tries to be everything in the business: visionary, office clerk, accountant, salesperson, cleaner, solicitor, etc. This model is hard to sustain as you are bound to get tired and deflated at some point. Also, what this means is your business cannot run if you are physically unavailable, and it will suffer.[16] An invaluable piece of advice I would recommend for anyone starting a business is to clearly outline your 'why' for starting the business, and always be systematic in your approach. Think of how you can outsource things you do not like or do not know how to do. Put checks and balances in place to ensure that your business can run even without you.

The arena of business, and particularly sales, is one that has produced some of the most successful and wealthiest people of all time. As a matter of fact, no business can thrive without sales. Sales, many times, is dependent on marketing. What many of us do not know is that we are all salespersons. If you reflect deeply, I am sure you will recall a recent memory of trying to sell an idea or product to your friend, spouse, children or colleagues. The only difference was that you were not trying to monetise it. We all need to become better at marketing and sales, but most importantly for people running businesses, if you want to thrive, consider hiring someone to do this if you cannot do it yourself.

Provision of Information

We live in the information age. Everyone wants to know what is happening, and fast. People don't have time for newspapers anymore; they want the news on their social media feeds as soon as possible. We don't have time to read manuals anymore; we just look for the how-to videos on YouTube. We may not realise this, but what most of these giant IT companies are selling to us is information. Take, for example, Facebook, Google or YouTube. They provide information in the form of news feeds, internet searches, adverts and even *how-to* videos, and we pay either directly or indirectly to get this information. If you think you access these services for free, think again. You indirectly pay for these as the services advertised on these platforms add the cost of advertising to the prices of their services which you use, meaning that you rarely, if ever, get anything for free.

How then does this relate to making your money work for you? Is this a call for all of us to create the next big thing in the IT world? Definitely not. I am only trying to make it clear that, in today's world, people will pay for information just as much as they will pay for either food, clothing or shelter. This evolving industry is commonly referred to as the 'knowledge industry.' The big question, therefore, is what is it that you know about, or know how to do, that a lot of people would also like to know? There are a variety of ways you can get this information out there. This book you are reading is one example; you, or someone else, probably paid to get a copy of this book.

You can set up classes and seminars as well. This can be done either in real-time (offline) or even online. The online option is more lucrative these days, because you have no limit to the space in your classroom. The possibilities are truly endless. Internet websites, blogsites, social media accounts, and YouTube channels are also other examples of how information provision could potentially earn you money. The more traffic or followers you can attract with the quality of information you provide, the more your chances of making money - either through adverts or plainly through networking. The evolution of technology in this day and time even makes it easier for you to access your specific kind of audience, however unique that might be, from the comfort of your living room. The best thing about this money-generating medium is that it does not require as much capital as most of the others I listed earlier. Most times, what it demands from you is time and serious thinking to create a quality product that delivers enough value that people would be willing to pay for.

There are many other avenues to make your money work for you, and I do not claim to know them all. The most important thing is to carry out due diligence in whatever venture you decide to go into, and look before you leap. You do not want a catastrophic accident to happen. Speak to certified financial advisers if you need to.

Learning from Practical Examples

Meet Dr Herbert Wertheim (1939-)

Herbert was born in May 1939 to Jewish refugees who fled Nazi Germany. They settled in Florida in 1945 and lived in an apartment above the family's bakery. Herbert was dyslexic and therefore struggled with school in early life, sometimes being referred to as dumb and having to wear a dunce cap in a corner of the class. He also had to run away from home sometimes as his father was abusive. He faced a judge for truancy charges at the age of 16, but the judge had mercy on him and gave him the option of joining the U.S Navy. It was in the Navy that his life changed, as several tests showed he was naturally good in the field of mechanics and organisation. He, therefore, went on to study Physics and Chemistry. It was also in the Navy that he made his first investment with his stipends at the age of 18, buying stocks in Lear Jet, an aviation company.[17]

After his time in the Navy, Herbert studied engineering and worked at NASA for a while, where he developed an interest in the eye and instruments optimised for vision. He later received a scholarship to study Optometry at the Southern College of Optometry in Memphis and thereafter started his optometry practice. During the years of his clinical optometry practice, he kept working in the evenings on inventing a tint for plastic lenses that would help prevent cataracts by absorbing ultraviolet rays from the sun. This invention became popular during the Vietnam war and earned Dr Wertheim some money. With this, he founded his own business called Brain Power Inc. that continues to manufacture optical tints for eyeglasses to this day.

Since 1970, Dr Wertheim has invested his profits from Brain Power Inc. in the stock market using low fee providers like Fidelity and Schwab, adopting a strategy of investing in only what he knows about. He has invested in Microsoft, Apple and many other tech firms including IBM, 3M and Intel. He also used his aeronautical knowledge to help a family with its management of Heico, their Aerospace business, which he invested in. He is currently its largest shareholder and his investment is worth over $800 million. His current net worth as at May 2020 is $2.75 billion.

Dr Wertheim has made substantial contributions to charitable organisations through the Dr Herbert and Nicole Wertheim Family Foundation. He has contributed to hundreds of local and international educational, sporting and healthcare organisations. He has given $50 million to Florida International University (FIU) and committed another $50 million to the University of Florida. He also pledged $25 million to the University of Florida to help create a school of public health. In June 2009, the FIU Board of Trustees named the new college the Herbert Wertheim College of Medicine in his honour, and named him Founding Chairman of the College of Medicine and Trustee Emeritus of the University. Herbie is also a signee to the Bill Gates and Warren Buffet Giving Pledge which is a commitment by some wealthy people of the world to give at least half of their net worth to philanthropy, either during their lifetime or upon their death.[18]

"Herbie Time," referring to his personal time, is this billionaire's favourite preoccupation at present. He spends many winters cruising with his wife and family on the most luxurious residential ship on the planet named *The World* where he owns two luxurious apartments. When reflecting on his long career and investment journey, Herbert remarked, "I wanted to be able to have free time. To me having time is the most precious thing."

Dr Wertheim, therefore, espouses what this chapter is all about. Why use all your time and energy to work for money, when you can get money to work for you so you can use your time and energy for what you love, while still contributing positively to the course of humanity?

Reflection and Action Steps

- How many years have you worked for in total? Multiply that by the number of hours you work per week and then by the number of weeks in a year. This should give a rough idea of how many hours you have worked in your lifetime.

- How many more hours do you think you have left in your lifetime?

- How long do you think you could survive if you were asked to stop working here and now?

- Have you ever made money that you did not work for? How did this feel?

- What do you think you can put your time and money into that can yield rewards a few years down the line?

- Do you need to learn about a business or the stock market? Have you ever considered going into real estate? What is stopping you?

- Register an account with a low fee index fund provider and start buying shares.

- Decide on the business sector you would like to enter into. Look for training in that sector and speak to people who you know are already in that sector.

- Approach your bank and enquire about business loans and ask if you are entitled to one.

- What is it that you know so much about that you can teach a group of people? Have you considered making a book or video or course out of this?

Chapter 6

Protect What You Love

Let us start this chapter with imagining a mother hen protecting her precious eggs. It is such a wonderful sight to behold. The mother hen takes care of, and keeps watch over, her eggs and would even fight anyone who tries to snatch her eggs away. Naturally, you would consider a hen that abandons its eggs and wanders around as completely unprofessional and irresponsible. Why then do we do the same thing as professionals? We all have people or things that we love; it could be our families, projects, businesses, or even material things like houses or cars, etc. We do not want to see any of these suffer or perish while we are here, or even after we are long gone. Many a professional, however, like an irresponsible mother hen, has consistently failed to protect what they love. We have heard stories of successful people who lost everything they had due to lawsuits, accidents, taxes, death, divorce, or ill-health, etc. In some cases, due to poor planning, their offspring never got access to all the wealth they accumulated over their lives. Do not get me wrong - I am not asking us to keep brooding over our belongings and investments all day long. What I am simply saying is there are some processes, sometimes automated, that we can use to protect these assets and help us get our well-deserved sleep.

A rich man from my home country was once famous for saying that his riches were so infinite that even if termites decided to invade his wealth, they would only eat so much and end up getting tired of eating. He is dead now and, last time I checked, his wealth and legacy have dwindled so much that it has become rather insignificant. Though his wealth was legitimate and his wealth-building strategies sound, he did not set enough checks and balances to ensure their preservation, long after he was gone. This brings us to the main focus of this chapter. How can you protect those you love, what you love, and what you worked so hard to earn?

Emergency Funds

If asked about the need for emergency funds, virtually everyone would agree they are an absolute necessity; but if we tried to find out how many of us truly have emergency funds, the answer would be a shocker. A study by Bankrate in the US in 2018 showed that 1 in every 4 Americans had no savings at all, and another quarter had less than 3 months' worth of expenses saved.[19] It also showed that it is the younger professionals who are more likely to have no savings at all. What was even more shocking was that 2 of every 3 Americans in this same study said they were comfortable with the amount of savings they had — most of which was little or nothing. The reason many people are comfortable with their lack of savings is due to their reliance on credit facilities, but I would like to tell you that this is not a sustainable approach. People of today's generation ask why we would ever need to stash some money away and how much is ever enough to save.

Emergency funds are funds saved in special accounts for unforeseen (and usually sudden) circumstances, which could range from minor things like a change of faulty household equipment or car repairs, to even more serious things like ill-health, accidents, short-term job loss or change. This is different from things that are traditionally covered by insurance, or money that is used for things like business and investments. In terms of the ideal amount needed in an emergency fund, most financial advisers recommend at least six months' worth of your monthly expenses. This assumes that in the event of unforeseen circumstances such as a job loss, six months should be sufficient time to find your footing and recover from the initial setback. If you, however, do not have this buffer in the form of emergency funds, you might have to face the harsh reality of embarrassing and painful times, or bear the brunt of high-interest rates from credit lenders. No one prays for hard times; however, just like winter comes after summer, everyone is likely to experience hard times at some point in their lives. Emergency funds will help you to truly sleep at night knowing that, if the winter comes, you have enough logs in the cabin to keep you warm. Another benefit of emergency funds, which is not commonly talked about, is that it gives you the confidence to go ahead and invest knowing that, if things do not go as well as planned, you (and your family) will not be stranded, since you have your lifeline saved securely elsewhere.

Retirement Pensions

When do you want to retire? What is holding you back now? Is it the love of your job or the fear of being idle? Is it because you do not have enough in your retirement pot, and have no idea how to sustain your living after you stop working? The average retirement age in most countries is 65. At this age, many people become either confused or worried, because they realise the pension contributions they relied on are not exactly what they hoped for; they probably cannot sustain the lives they had always dreamed of after retirement. Therefore, we find many professionals getting back to their jobs to sustain their livelihoods. The original pensions plan was effective when people's needs were not as numerous as today, and life expectancy was not as long as it is now. Nowadays even elderly people want to have the best things in life, drive posh cars, go on trips around the world, play golf and still give to their heirs. Advances in medical care mean people are living for many years after their retirement age. To complicate the pensions scenario, most governments have not been handling the largest money pot in the world well over time, as it is becoming evident that pensions, as we know them, are beginning to fail and may not be sustainable. Many young professionals today, therefore, have the hidden fear of outliving their contributions when they retire, but this can be prevented if we take the right steps in our early years.

To start with, you can increase your pension contributions, and this is a wise choice if you work with an organisation that matches your pension contribution. This means for every extra penny you put into your pension, your employer adds the same amount to your pension pot for you. Sounds unbelievable, right? Well, it is true and it is free money for you to maximise if you have access to this feature. Another clever thing to do with regards to your pensions is to apply and contribute to another private pension of your own choice, separate from what your employer provides. Hence when you hit retirement age, you get pension payments from both sources. Sometimes, this might not be a tax-efficient option depending on the country you reside in; hence I would advise you to check with a tax adviser.

Also, with some pension agencies, it is possible to control where the money in your pensions pot is invested. While this option seems lucrative, I would advise this only for people who have an experience of investing. Flip back to the section on investing if this does not apply to you. You do not want to lose all your pension money by making the wrong investment choices. This is another reason why I encourage you to be a seasoned investor. Understanding the investment process gives you more confidence if you decide to take the self-investing option which, if well done, could be a sound financial decision.

Insurance

The principle of insurance is simple. For a small subscription, protect yourself against the unforeseen, unlikely mishap. Many of these things never happen but, once in a while, they do. I remember once when I cancelled the repair and support insurance for my personal computer, I felt like I had made the right move and was a winner. Shortly after, however, my computer developed issues and when I took it back to the store I was told I had to pay a high price to get it fixed. If nothing had happened to the laptop, I would have deemed myself to be smart, but unfortunately, since something went wrong with it, I felt I had shot myself in the foot. Since then, I always learned to think twice before refusing to insure, or cancelling insurance, on something of potential value to me. You can insure virtually anything in today's world and rightly selected insurance pays off.

Someone once asked me to name one thing that was sure to happen to everyone, like 100% of the time. I did not have to think too much to know the answer was 'Death.' Yes, everyone will die and it is rather surprising that, while we insure many of our possessions against unlikely events, many of us professionals refuse to insure ourselves against the one very certain thing - death. Doesn't sound professional, does it? This is a big issue for most people, especially the young, as we think of death as a long way ahead - but you never can tell. I am sure we all know someone, a family member or a friend, who died unexpectedly at a young age. Life Insurance should be an absolute necessity for everyone in a working age group, and even more importantly for those of us who have dependants. This way, you rest assured that if anything happens to you and you have to leave this world prematurely, those who you love will not have to suffer. Other valuable forms of insurance to consider, especially for working professionals, are income protection cover — which pays a certain percentage of your income monthly for a specified period if you lose your ability to work due to an illness or injury - and critical illness cover, which pays a lump sum if you are diagnosed with any of the medical conditions listed by your insurer as critical illnesses. These will ensure you remain financially safe if you lose your job or the ability to work due to an illness or injury, as we have seen happen to other professionals before.

Estate Planning

A step further from insurance is estate planning. What do you want to happen to all of your wealth when you are gone? How do you want it to be managed? Do you want all your wealth to be disputed by your family for many years after you die? Successful people take estate planning seriously because they understand how hard they worked to gather what they did all through their lifetime, and do not want it to be wasted by anyone - not even their children, or the government.

The first basic step in estate planning is writing your will. Many of us get cold shivers or goosebumps when we hear that word "will." A survey of 2,000 people done in the UK by Macmillan Cancer Support revealed that nearly two-thirds of adults do not have a will in place.[20] But a will is only what it is — writing showing how you want your properties to be allocated when you die. It does not shorten your lifespan in any way. If anything, it helps you to reflect on your life and achievements so far, and could be a positive motivational factor. It is important to know that this document can be reviewed from time to time, so it does not have to be a 'get it right once-and-for-all affair.' Many people push the idea of writing a will to some other time in the future, simply because they think they do not have enough to pass on. Writing a will when you think you don't have enough leads to you to "count your blessings" - a process which many find rewarding as they realise they have more than they thought. This process also motivates you to work smarter, and sometimes harder, to increase the valuable store you are leaving behind. The unacceptable, unprofessional thing to do is to die without leaving a will behind, especially if you are married, have kids or have a positive net worth. This could mean your possessions will be managed and distributed according to the law, and not according to your wishes. It may also mean that your possessions may end up with someone who you did not want to have access to your property, or that someone you intended to give part of your possessions gets nothing at all.

Another main reason people do not consider writing a will is that they fear the legal costs; but some people find they are way cheaper than they thought they were. You can write your own will yourself, but I would not advise this as it can cost your family in terms of time, aggravation and excess legal fees if not properly done. I recently called the solicitor after I decided to write my own will, and I was really surprised at how uncomplicated the process was. All it took was two phone discussions with the solicitor – one with myself and the other with my wife - after which the will was drafted for us, and we got it signed and witnessed. What was more surprising was that we got it done for free as a national charity organisation sponsored the cost. Even if it wasn't free, for many of us getting a professional will done would probably be far cheaper than the cost of the next major holiday, so why not take a trip to the solicitor instead?

A step further in estate planning is estate or inheritance tax planning. This might not be for everyone reading this book presently, as it only applies to high net worth individuals whose wealth after passing on is subject to a significant level of taxation. If you fall into this category, it is worth speaking to your solicitor about this, as they can advise on specific things you can do such as leaving everything above the estate or inheritance tax threshold to your civil partner, spouse or a designated charity. You can also pay into a pensions account or set up trusts for your heirs. Many people find this rewarding, as knowing where their extra money goes is more reassuring than leaving it to the government, whose handling you can never predict.

Learning from Practical Examples

Meet Warren Buffett (1930-)

Warren was born in Omaha, Nebraska in 1930 to Leila Buffett (a homemaker) and Howard Buffett (a stockbroker who later served as a Congressman). He is considered by many to be the most successful investor of the 21st century. His primary investment vehicle, Berkshire Hathaway, owns more than 60 companies - including Duracell, the battery company, and Geico, the insurer. He was named the richest man in the world in 2008 and as of May 2020 is worth $69.2 billion.[21]

Warren has been known to demonstrate sound financial and business acumen since childhood. He made his first investment at the age of 11 when he bought three Cities Services shares at $38 per share. By the age of 13, he was already running his own business. Warren operates a principle called Value Investing which he learned from his mentor Benjamin Graham. His company's investment portfolio includes holdings in well-known companies such as Coca Cola, Bank of America and Apple Inc. In 2010, he was named in the Foreign Policy 2010 Report as the Most Influential Global Thinker, in conjunction with Bill Gates. In 2011, he was awarded the Presidential Medal of Freedom by President Barack Obama.

I have decided to highlight Warren in this chapter because of how he has successfully planned what would happen to his fortune after his death. Although Warren is one of the richest men in the world today, he has decided to donate up to 99% of his wealth to charity, most notably the Bill & Melinda Gates Foundation. He has instructed his will executors not to sell his shares but to rather give them away through annual gifts, 10 years after he has passed away. This saves him from having to pay capital gains tax from the sale of the shares. Rather, he would get charitable deductions based on the fair value of the stock. This demonstrates prudent financial planning.

Warren believes in self-sufficiency and promotes good work ethics in his family so, unlike most people, he has no plans of leaving his inheritance to his children. The remaining 1% which he is leaving behind for his wife is still a significant amount of money, and being the financially savvy person that he is, he has made plans for even this money. He has advised that 10% of this be used to purchase government-backed bonds and the remaining 90% be invested in passively managed low-cost index funds.[22] This is because he believes index funds would do better than any portfolio manager or financial planner in the long run.

The purpose of this example is not to get you to design your estate and inheritance plans like Warren Buffet's. The aim is to highlight the importance of having plans for your money while you are still here, and even after you leave. After all, you have worked for or earned it over the years, so you should have a say regarding how it should be put to good use.

Reflection and Action Steps

- Do you have funds saved up in case an emergency showed up right now? If not, what is your back-up?

- Do you have anything valuable to leave behind to your family if you suddenly died today? Have you made arrangements for how this would be distributed?

- How are you going to make sure your possessions are passed on with the least tax implications for your family? How would you ensure the assets are put to good use for future generations?

- Consider speaking to a solicitor to find out the cost and process of writing a will today.

- Check with your employer what their policy on pensions is. Can you maximise pension contributions?

- Find out how much you will be paid monthly upon retirement based on your current pension contribution. Would this amount be sufficient to cover your expenses and lifestyle?

- Does your employer offer any pay-out in the event of a death in service?

- Are you or your family covered in the event of inability to work, or death? Have you considered the options of income protection or life insurance?

Chapter 7

Knowledge Versus Action

Knowledge, they say, is power. Simply put, if you gather all the necessary or important knowledge you need in life, you have the power to create the life you want to live. Confucius is credited for saying the essence of knowledge is having it to use it. But how do we use the knowledge we have? The great scientist Isaac Newton stated in his third law of motion that "An object continues in a state of rest or uniform motion unless acted upon by an external force." This external force is what I would refer to as ACTION. It is therefore important to realise that knowledge gives you so much potential (energy) but you are likely to remain in your situation, not starting or stopping the things you need to, unless you give yourself that massive push and take action.

If it is as simple as it seems, why then do people not take action? I suppose the major reason people do not act is because they perceive it as 'risky.' We are used to the status quo and we feel any disturbance to the balance of the forces of nature is likely to lead us into something we are not sure of. A trip into the uncertain or unsure is deemed risky, and many times this leads us to avoid acting.

I would like to propose here that knowledge, risk and action are all interconnected. Generally, the more we know about a venture or procedure, the less risky we deem it to be. For example, think of a surgeon who knows he has mastered his skill over time, and who would generally know how to eliminate or potentially reduce risks during surgeries in a way that amateurs do not. It would not be surprising therefore to find that such a surgeon can act when it comes to the most challenging and daunting operations, which most amateurs would shy away from.

But would this surgeon go ahead with all operations? Definitely not! The best surgeons, who coincidentally have the best outcomes, are those who choose their procedures carefully. This isn't purely because they can reduce risks, but also because they have been trained to identify and steer clear from hazardous risks. Amateurs, however, cannot identify them and end up with the poorer outcomes. This analogy holds true for almost every sphere of life. The major problem for many of us, therefore, isn't the presence of risks, but the inability to identify them. If we transfer this illustration to a venture like stock market trading, you will agree with me that most of us generally avoid the stock market simply because we don't know well enough to identify risky stocks or shares, and so we do not take action.

The more we learn about what we want to venture into, the better we are at identifying hazardous risks, and ultimately the easier it will be to take positive action. My advice, therefore, as other chapters in this book will continue to echo, is to invest some time, effort and possibly resources in getting knowledge and experience in the things that matter.

I remember taking a real estate training course some time ago. The more I learnt on the course, the easier it was for me to identify deals that were potentially risky, as the numbers did not work. The ability to identify such risks gave me the confidence to make positive moves, such as setting up a company, visiting estate agents and holding meetings with mortgage brokers, lending agencies and accountants, and viewing and putting offers up for properties; things I would never have done if I was still clouded by the fear of unknown risks. These positive moves paid off and are still reaping good rewards.

Another helpful approach in reducing risks and encouraging meaningful action is to look for a mentor. This can be anyone, but ideally should be someone who has done what you intend to do before and has succeeded at it. Your mentor will know the pitfalls to avoid and the right people you need to meet, and can sometimes lead you along the way. This is not to say that you cannot learn things on your own by trial and error, but the help of a mentor can make the process faster. Another advantage of having a mentor is that having someone you are accountable to encourages discipline, and your mentor can sometimes actually push you to make the right moves, if necessary, when you are held back by inertia. If you have a venture that you have considered for a long time but haven't made a move, then you may want to get yourself a mentor - even if means you have to pay for it.

Here comes the big question: which is more important, knowledge or action?

A glance at the title of this book might make you believe I would go for knowledge over action. However, I would not! I believe positive action trumps knowledge most of the time. Too much of knowledge has been shown sometimes to cause what many describe as 'analysis paralysis.' When you know too much about the venture, it could cause you to overanalyse everything that can go wrong, and wait for all the stars in the sky to align in your favour before you make a move. The truth is that this might go on forever and you might never make a move. In contrast, someone without knowledge that takes positive action has variable chances of either succeeding or failing depending on what venture he or she has embarked upon. While it might be disastrous to make mistakes and fail, the good thing is that we learn from it and ultimately, as long as the individual is willing to keep pushing, there is a better chance of succeeding on further attempts because this time around action will be combined with some experiential knowledge. As Donald Trump once said, the biggest risk we all face is in not moving forward with what we have learned.

A good example of this concept can be drawn from the days when I thought about writing this book. I knew there was a lot I did not know, so I did not start writing immediately. At the same time, I knew learning all I needed to write a bestseller that would educate professionals from all fields of life would take forever. It dawned on me along the line that you do not have to be perfect to get started. Perfection, many times, is the enemy of progress. Mastery is a process that takes time. I, therefore, got to learn some of the concepts I have talked about in this book, but did not wait to learn them all. Instead, I just started and, truthfully, I have had to discard some of the stuff I wrote in the early days as my knowledge increased; but I am grateful I didn't wait to learn it all before I started, otherwise I probably wouldn't have written a word.

This brings me to my conclusion on this chapter: action without knowledge is risky, but knowledge without action is useless. Knowledge is universal. The difference lies in how we apply it. Action with some useful knowledge is optimal for success. They work synergistically and not in isolation. You don't need to know it all at the beginning. Just like the Nike popular trademark, once you have foundation knowledge on what you want to do, JUST DO IT!

Learning from Practical Examples

Meet Jack Ma (1964-)

Jack Ma, originally known as Ma Yun, was born to a poor family in Hangzhou in 1964. Despite facing several setbacks in life, he has been able to rise from being a poor child to an English teacher, and thereafter a Tech billionaire.

Jack has always been known to take action when the opportunity arises. The boost in tourism when former US President Nixon visited Hangzhou stimulated Jack's interest in the English language. He was known to wake up and arrive early at the tourist hotels, offering free tours to foreigners in exchange for English lessons. He later went on to study English language and worked as a teacher in Hangzhou Danzi University.[23]

Jack's actions did not always yield positive results, and he has faced rejection and failure several times in his life. He once applied for a job when KFC first came to China and, of the 24 people that applied, he was the only one rejected.[23] He also applied to Harvard University ten times and was rejected every single time. He also had a shot at entrepreneurship and his first two ventures failed.

Jack's breakthrough came in 1995 when he had an opportunity to visit the United States on behalf of Hangzhou city government, during which he discovered the Internet. Although he had no experience or training in computer or programming, and had never been successful at sales, he yet saw a big opportunity in facilitating Chinese trade through the internet, which was largely unpopular before then. He managed to

convince a group of friends to invest and join his new start-up -
which he named AliBaba.

AliBaba grew and in 2005, Yahoo offered $1 billion in exchange
for a 40% stake in the company. In 2014, the company debuted
an initial public offering at the New York Stock exchange, raising
capital of $21.8 billion for the company.[24] Jack Ma still holds a
7.8% stake in AliBaba and a 50% stake in AliPay, the company's
payment processing service. He is officially one of the richest men
in China with a net worth of $41.3 billion in 2020.[25]

Jack Ma's story demonstrates to us that taking action despite
previous failures or lack of experience is a key ingredient for
success. We need to reduce the gap between the conception of an
idea and the time it takes for execution. As Jack loves to say, when
you get opportunities like this, "Go big or go home."

Reflection and Action Steps

- What area of your life have you gathered knowledge in over the years that you haven't taken any action on?

- Have you ever had an opportunity taken away from you before because you thought too long about it?

- What's your definition of risk? Have you done anything you considered risky before? How did it feel?

- Have you ever failed at something before because you didn't know enough about it? Did you learn anything from this experience?

- Have you ever experienced mentorship in an area of life? Did you find it helpful?

- Write down one thing you would do if you were told it was impossible to fail at it.

- Speak to someone you know that has succeeded at this venture before. Consider enlisting the help or services of a mentor.

- Do something you have never done before.

Chapter 8

Maximising Your Productivity

We are all made up of millions of energy-producing molecules – protons, neutrons and electrons. To think that I utterly dislike physics and yet I am about to use another of Newton's laws, is rather unimaginable. I, however, think this is important at this stage, so I will use it anyway. Newton's Law of Conservation of Energy states that energy is neither created nor destroyed; rather it is only transformed from one form to the other. You might be wondering what all this science has got to do with taking charge of your life. Remember earlier in this book, we talked about the *must-knows* and the *good-to-knows?* Similarly, there are the *must-dos* and *good-to-dos.*

We all live in a fast-paced world where there is so much pressure to get things done in the space of very little time. To make things even more complicated, we are all finite and mortal beings. I believe that even Superman is only just another man. We all need to recognise that we have limits and work within the reasonable confines of our limits. The type of energy I want to focus on in this chapter is mental energy. This is because this form of energy is what will determine what you can achieve and your state of well-being, at least while you are here on this earth. We might have noticed that some people tend to achieve more than others; we wonder how they accomplish such feats and may sometimes be tempted to get jealous of such people. Their real secret is not necessarily that they have more energy than the rest of us; rather it is that they have learnt to channel their energy towards the attainment of goal-oriented tasks.

I confess that I never really liked Physics and I imagine some of us are in the same boat. However, I assume many of us would be able to relate to the fact that efficiency, or productivity, is a function of energy and time. If it takes one man one hour to get a job done and another man does the same job in 10 minutes, then we can say that the second man is more productive. But it doesn't just end with the second man being productive; the added advantage is that he still has fifty minutes spare to do something else. And the more he does with this 'spare time,' the more productive he becomes. This brings us to the two major concepts in this chapter - controlling your time and channelling your energy.

Controlling your time

I always believed that everyone has the same time (twenty-four hours a day) and that time once spent is never regained. While this is true on the face of it, a closer look would make you realise this isn't entirely true. What is important is the amount of time you have for yourself, for your dreams, aspirations and goals. If you agree that we all need to get some sleep every day and look at time in this context, you will understand that some people have absolutely no time at all, while some might have up to 12 hours a day. The people who do not have any time at all are not necessarily lazy people or time-wasters. Their time is mostly taken up by legitimate tasks such as their day job, commuting in traffic, looking after the family, house chores and other tasks.

The most successful people in life have developed mechanisms to protect or buy back their time. A major strategy that can help you to buy back your time is to determine what is urgent and what is important. You will realise that most of the activities you have to do will fall under one of these quadrants of the Time Management Matrix:

a. Important and urgent

Things under this category could be drafting a business plan, or delivering a client's job on time, or getting an assignment with a deadline done; or it can even be very straightforward things like going on your morning run or having your daily reflection session. These are usually things that, for the most part, have to be done by you and you alone. Most productive and successful people focus on this and ensure they get it done with the least possible interruption. For this group of activities, the best advice is 'Do them now.'

b. Important but not urgent

There are some things in life that are utterly important but might not be so urgent. A practical example would be a family vacation or a golf game with your business partners. You will agree with me that these are important things to be done, but can be done later. Following a thoughtful discussion with the concerned parties, the best advice for this group of activities is to draft up a plan to do them later, and please ensure you keep to your word and stick to this plan.

These 'important things' - whether urgent or not, are usually the essential ingredients for success in life. They are very often the most ignored or postponed by unsuccessful people. A critical factor in ensuring your success in life is in identifying what the important things in your life are, and ensuring you are accountable for getting them done. If not, they will be filled with the unimportant things, simply because nature abhors a vacuum; if you don't fill your schedule with the right stuff, you will automatically get a busy schedule filled with all the unimportant things.

C. Not important but urgent

This is one of the areas where mediocre people fail, but rich people have learnt to master. You need to realise that you don't necessarily have to do everything yourself. You might agree that sometimes menial tasks, such as laundry, mowing the lawn or doing the dishes, might come to a point where it becomes critically urgent, otherwise, all hell will let loose in your home or your wardrobe! Yet these tasks aren't necessarily important. Sometimes we get stuck trying to do these things, especially with our DIY mentality, and we waste so much potentially valuable time in accomplishing them that we end up with very little time to do the important things. The rich and successful have learnt to buy back their time by getting, or paying, someone else to do these so they can focus on more important tasks. Many people would argue that this is a waste of money, as paying would eat up a considerable chunk of your savings. But if you were to focus on using the freed time for income or result-generating tasks rather than just leisure or lazing around, you would realise that this is an ultimate game-changer. I call it being 'pound wise rather than penny foolish.' To summarise, for this group of activities that are urgent but not important, the best decision is to 'delegate them to someone else.'

D. Not important, not urgent

This category differs from person to person, as what's important for someone might not necessarily be important for another. I would give examples of what I consider as unimportant for me, but I'd like to plead that no one is offended by my choices as you may consider this important for you. What matters is self-awareness and realising what isn't important or urgent. I love the game of football, and I love playing games or sitting and watching a good movie. Although these might be pleasurable things to do, I know they are neither important nor urgent for me, as leaving them till a later date or time is unlikely to have negative consequences on my productivity. I would only consider these things when I have sorted out issues in the other three quadrants and still have spare time left. In the beginning, it seems impossible to do without these things, but all it takes is one singular action after the other. It might just be cancelling a subscription or deleting an app. Once you start, you discover it is not as difficult as you had always thought. For unimportant and not so urgent tasks or pleasures, I would like to advise you to kindly 'defer them,' sometimes indefinitely!

Channelling your energy

Staying on the subject of energy, we would agree that we all have different forms of energy - physical energy, spiritual energy, mental energy, emotional energy. Like I said earlier in the chapter, we do not necessarily create these forms of energy but can transform them from one form to the other. We need to understand as individuals that we are multi-dimensional - having a body, soul, spirit and mind. Have you noticed that the most successful people in the world tend to have most, if not all, of these forms of energy at above-average levels?

Similarly, people who have low energy levels in these dimensions - for example, by being unhealthy or overweight, lacking spiritual identity or commitment, being depressed or emotionally unstable, as well as sexually insecure or unstable - are more likely to end up being unsuccessful. Most successful people know that their energy forms are connected, and that is why they do what is necessary to stay high in these dimensions. The late motivational speaker Jim Rohn popularly used to say, "Every discipline affects every other discipline." For example, an individual can rev up his physical energy in the morning by going on a run, boost his spiritual energy by being thankful and saying a prayer, listening to a motivational message on his way out to prime his mental energy, and carrying on with the day by translating these forms of energy from one to the other as and when needed. However, if you are low in many of these dimensions, you eventually end up low in all as there is virtually no energy to transform to undertake the productive tasks necessary in life to become successful.

I chose to mention these dimensions because you need to be careful of the potential things that can drain your energy and hinder your path to success. Just think of the dimensions and you can easily come up with 'energy drainers' that can ultimately hinder your productivity. Examples would include things like unhealthy eating and morbid obesity, depression, worry and fear, sexual insecurity, and spiritual crises. Having any of these things doesn't necessarily mean that you cannot attain success, but it can also significantly hinder your success or make your success less enjoyable. The reason I have highlighted these energy drainers is to encourage you to eliminate them as much as possible, as this will improve your energy and productivity, and ultimately your chances for life-changing success.

An important factor in being able to channel your energy is also knowing when you are most productive, i.e. recognising when you are at your peak state. It is commonly said that the most successful people always wake up very early in the morning. However, this is not always the case. Some people are at their peak in the morning - they can work-out, prepare for the day, read and meditate in the early hours of the day. I like to refer to these people as 'morning crows.' These people cannot function well at night, and if they are overstretched into the night, they are as good as useless. For such people, they must get their work done early enough during the day so that they do the less brain-taxing activities as the day draws to a close, then get into bed early enough so they can rise early enough for another productive morning.

On the other hand, there is another group of people, which I call the 'night owls,' who are most productive late into the night when everyone is asleep. Naturally, they don't wake up early during the day and, even if they do, cannot function well. For such people waking up late is important as they usually sleep late into the night. Most people fall into either of these categories, and it is important you recognise which defines you better. An added advantage of these times of the day is that there is the least distraction, making it easier to complete tasks. The combination of your peak state with the absence of distractions can be an ultimate game-changer in your productivity journey. So once again, I would encourage you to identify what works for you and stick to it. While doing this, ensure you get adequate rest, as confusing your natural body rhythm (circadian rhythm) can be stressful for your body and impact on your productivity negatively.

Learning from Practical Examples

Meet Sir Richard Branson (1950-)

Sir Richard Branson was born in London in 1950. He is a business magnate, author, investor and philanthropist. He is the founder of the Virgin Group that controls over 400 companies in various fields, including telecommunications, aviation, music, retail and finance. Despite being dyslexic, he is one of the most respected entrepreneurs in the world. According to Forbes, he has a net worth of about $5 billion. Sir Branson is not only famous for his wealth, but also for his globetrotting adventures and casual attitude. So how does Sir Branson manage to live such an adventurous life and combine running over 400 companies?

Sir Branson wakes up at 5 am every day and starts his day with some form of exercise: walking, running, cycling or surfing. Afterwards, he sits to have some family time over breakfast. He attests this not only helps his family know how important they are to him, but also helps put him in a great frame of mind before getting down to business. Mr Branson's structured morning routine helps him to focus and achieve the things he needs to.

The next thing he does is power through his emails before most of the world is awake. Having to respond to 300 to 400 emails every day is also not an easy task, so he goes through them in bursts, sometimes having to dictate replies for his assistants or delegate this task to someone else. Mr Branson spends most of his workday staying on top of business, checking his various social media platforms and communicating with his teams all over the world.[26]

Mr Branson says his secret life hack is his pen and notebook, which he always has with him to write down ideas as soon as they come to him. He also writes down tasks and organises them in order of importance and urgency, and he says this helps to keep him on track. He has also written many bestseller books.

Although Mr Branson has had several near-death experiences on many of his adventures, he is by no means a superhero and admits running over 400 companies all by himself is impossible. He has a knack of surrounding himself with extremely talented people who support his vision, and delegates tasks to them. Despite being an extremely successful businessman, Sir Branson has also, over time, learnt to say no to some ventures. A notable example is from the Virgin Films project which started about the same time as Virgin Atlantic. The Virgin Films project proved too risky to dedicate time and money to as he and his team were trying to get the Virgin Atlantic business going, and he had to walk away from it.

Mr Branson is not a big TV watcher, but enjoys the occasional movie. To help him stay focused during the day, he practises Yoga and Tai Chi. He also drinks a lot of tea without sugar to stay energised. He has dinner with family and friends and settles to bed around 11 pm to get about 6 hours of sleep, before he starts the next day with the same routine. [27]

There is so much to learn about maximising our productivity from this business magnate, including maximising and transforming our energy through our routines and activities, organising our tasks in order of importance and urgency, delegating tasks and learning to say no when necessary.

Reflection and Action Steps

- How much time in a day do you have for yourself? Take note of the time you use for things like work, commuting, eating, sleeping, chores and family.

- If you were to insert the activities you use your time for into the four quadrants, which of the quadrants would they fall into?

- Are there things that you can save time on because they are neither important nor urgent? Is it possible to delegate or hire some of these services?

- What time of the day are you most productive? Do you use this time for your most important tasks? Study your pattern and attempt doing your most important tasks during this time.

- Do you feel full of energy or low in energy on most days?

- Does your energy level affect more than one aspect of your life? Reflect on a previous time when being low in one aspect played out on other aspects of your life. What can you learn from this?

- Which activities have you noticed make you feel livelier and more energetic? Make a plan to do more of these activities.

Chapter 9

Look After the Vessel

In my first full write-up of this book, I didn't include this chapter. However, I considered it unfair not to talk about this given how important it is to our lives, and the background knowledge I have in this field. As I have reiterated several times in this book, we human beings are multi-dimensional - and one of the dimensions is our physical bodies and health. We all must have experienced a period of illness at some point in our lives, and we can attest it practically knocks us off in all other dimensions. If an individual has a debilitating illness, while it doesn't make it impossible to live a successful life you will agree with me that it would be more difficult compared to another, healthy, individual.

This is because, as I explained in the previous chapter on maximising productivity, we transform energy from one form to another. Someone unwell is low in physical energy and therefore cannot muster up enough mental and emotional energy necessary to engage in the activities necessary for success. There are, however, some truly exceptional people who have been able to achieve high levels of success despite their physical limitations. For this reason, we must learn how to look after our bodies as well. Motivational speaker Les Brown puts it this way: "You have only one body, so why won't you look after it?"

Many years ago, most of the diseases we needed to battle as humans were infectious and communicable diseases; things like Malaria, Polio, Chicken pox, and Tuberculosis to name a few. However, with the increasing research and development, the advent of antibiotics, improved hygiene and sanitary practices, many of these diseases are gradually being eradicated or controlled in some regions. Even more recent evolutions of viral illnesses like HIV and Viral Hepatitis have been fought with antiviral agents that effectively control the replication of these viruses so individuals can live normal, or near-normal, lives. Many more people are therefore living to ripe old ages before dying. Naturally, this should mean the victory of the human race against diseases, but we are still left with the scourge of non-communicable diseases in the present world; one that poses a challenge even greater than the one we faced from infectious and communicable diseases.

Today's rising disease burden includes diseases like Cancers, cardiovascular diseases like Strokes and Heart attacks, and more commonly a group of Autoimmune diseases where the body is effectively recognising its cells and tissues as foreign and fighting them. Although many of these diseases have been in existence for a long time, I would like to argue that they are becoming more common in our lifetime, and even affecting younger individuals by the day. What is the cause of all of these? Is it a by-product of man's industrial revolution and impact on the environment? The truth is that I do not know. Perhaps if as medical professionals we knew the causes of all of these, then it would be easy to solve them by simply removing the causes. What we know, however, is that there are certain things or situations that put one more at risk. We have also found that addressing these issues in people who have already developed these diseases improves their condition, or their chances of survival at least. I recently attended a conference filled with heart specialists, and an important issue was raised which I think is an important issue for all of us to ponder upon. The issue stemmed from a question which was asked: "Why are we so big on newer treatments for diseases such as heart disease, diabetes, hypertension, etc. when we can gain a lot more by focusing on their prevention?"

The truth is that our shortcut or fast-lane lifestyle in our present generation has also eroded our health. There are millions of people who are on anti-hypertensive and anti-diabetic medications when we know that healthy diets and regular exercise could have prevented these diseases from occurring and could also be beneficial in their treatment. There is also a similar number of people on cholesterol-lowering drugs rather than cutting down on their dietary intake of unhealthy foods. A large number of people are waiting in line to have stents in their hearts when measures like avoiding cigarette smoking or stopping altogether, living active lives and good nutrition could have helped ensure that our coronary arteries remain in good condition. These preventative measures are therefore things I would encourage everyone to do, and will be the focus of this chapter.

Physical Exercise

We cannot over-emphasize the importance of physical exercise to our health as human beings. A product of civilisation is that we now do less physical activity than we used to. Think about it: we no longer have to use the stairs, we have elevators; we no longer have to walk for miles as that is what cars were made for; We don't have to hunt and cook food for hours - that's the reason fast-food was invented. While I am thankful for all these technological advancements, as I cannot imagine what life would be without them, it still does not undermine the fact that it has taken a vital activity from us - physical activity. What we can do in this age and time is to ensure we keep up with regular physical activity through exercise. The timing, duration and frequency of this is entirely up to you, as any exercise is better than no exercise at all.

During exercise, your heart pumps out blood faster and harder than usual, improving circulation as well as the elimination of toxins from your entire body. Exercise also helps to control our body weight, hence reducing the risk of diseases associated with being overweight. Also, physical activity has been shown to improve our mental energy and mood, which correlates with my earlier proposition that energy is transformed from one form to another. What's there to lose by exercising? I recommend you start today if you haven't done so already.

Concerning diseases, I can summarise the benefits of exercise as follows: it reduces your chances of being sick, and even if you unfortunately get sick, it increases your chances of recovery, and also increases your chances of being offered the best form of treatment available. Whatever the case, therefore, exercising always remains a win-win scenario for you.

Avoidance of Toxic Substances

There are a number of man-made toxins that have been introduced into our lifestyle over time. Two of the most significant of these are alcohol and tobacco. It is undeniable that many of these are enjoyable indulgences, but it is also well known that they are linked to many of the non-communicable diseases we have in our lives today. Smoking is a greater culprit as it has a definite link with many cancers, respiratory and cardiovascular diseases. Current medical guidelines recommend individuals to stop smoking completely. For alcohol, the standpoint is still quite controversial. Some medical experts say moderate alcohol intake may be beneficial, although alcohol intake has been linked to many diseases as well. At present, guidelines recommend no more than 14 units of alcohol per week for both men and women. As one of my favourite quotes from Democritus says, "Throw moderation to the winds and the greatest pleasures bring the greatest pains." With a substance like alcohol which has addictive features or tendency for dependence, how then do we define moderation? Even the recommendations by health experts keep being updated, with different values being quoted as the recommended intake for males or females, so I would advise you tread carefully with regards to the type or quantity of alcohol you consume. We can argue there are millions of people who use these products all their lives without any significant consequences, but research has shown that there might be some genetic factors which 'protected' them from the dangerous effects of these substances. But then who knows whose genes are less susceptible or not? There are many other substances which are dangerous to our bodies, ranging from illegal drugs, chemicals, and radiation, to name a few. While scientists keep discovering new ones, for the well-known and established harmful substances, avoid them as much as possible.

Stress Management

It is well known that a little amount of stress sometimes helps to bring out a positive response in us. Whether it be deadlines at work, or upcoming exams, or a financial target, or even sudden danger. These short bursts of stress help our bodies produce stress hormones that help us increase our physiological response in the short term, such as increasing our heart rate, increasing our alertness and reducing our need for sleep. These are very helpful in the short term to overcome sudden danger or achieve needed results. For this reason, I will not say to avoid stress, as is commonplace. The problem, however, arises when a state of stress becomes a chronic or permanent situation. This leads to an alteration of the physiological and hormonal status of an individual producing disease. A lot of the diseases we encounter today can be linked to constant and chronic exposure to stressors, including but not limited to cardiovascular diseases, autoimmune and endocrine problems. Some studies have shown that when people are stressed and or depressed their immune system follows suit. If you find you are constantly in this state of exposure to stress, I recommend you take a break from the hustle and bustle, and get some good rest for your body and mind. Taking well-timed breaks can help to improve your physical and mental health, as well and ultimately boost your productivity. Do not deprive yourself of quality sleep. Routines like meditation and yoga work on the same principle and can be helpful.

Some recent interesting studies are also beginning to suggest that probably more important than the exposure to stress is the way we respond to stress. A leading Stanford psychologist reports that if people embrace the concept of stress, it can make them stronger, smarter and happier. This mindset, which involves viewing stress as a helpful part of life rather than as harmful, has been reported to be associated with better health, emotional well-being and productivity.[29] As the ancient Greek philosopher Epictetus once said, "It is not what happens to you, but how you react to it that matters." Permit yourself to smile or even laugh when things do not seem to be going your way; by finding some meaning through the stress, you can reduce the harmful effect of the stressors.

Healthy Nutrition

Our physical, and even mental, health relies heavily on what we eat. It depends on what kind of food we eat and how much we eat. With regards to what we eat, we should eat varied and balanced meals comprising the different classes of foods, i.e. carbohydrates, proteins, fats, minerals and vitamins and water, in the right proportions. Most foods consist of a mixture of these in different proportions, so if you try to eat a different meal from time to time, ultimately you will be getting these different classes of nutrients into your system. The important thing is to eat natural foods as much as possible - the more natural your meals, the more likely you will be getting these nutrients in the easily absorbable form. An unfortunate effect of civilisation is that we are having less and less of these natural foods on our plates, and replacing them with processed foods and drinks such as fizzy drinks, crisps, biscuits, cakes, and fries - only to mention a few.

Many of these processed foods contain some products that have been proven to harm our health if taken in excessive quantities — sugars, salt and saturated fats. For many people, these processed foods have become the staple food and the body takes a hit from these daily. We rarely get fruits and vegetables advertised to us as much as these processed foods that are dangled right in our faces. It is not rocket science: if you want to keep your body and mind healthy, you need to increase your intake of natural foods, including fruits and vegetables, and reduce your consumption of processed foods. Don't get me wrong — it is alright to have these processed foods once in a while; making them your regular diet is what I am against, as this is unhealthy. A simple hack which some people have found useful is to avoid these processed foods for most of the week, except on one day of the week called the 'cheat day.' On this day, they get to enjoy these processed foods. This might not be appropriate for everyone, but at least it reduces the intake to only one-seventh of the weekly intake, which is a fair amount.

Just as important as what you eat is how much you eat. Even if you only ate fruits and vegetables, eating too much of them can be unhealthy. You should eat just what is enough to keep you from feeling hungry. Many of us probably recall a time we had a bit too much to eat. How did we feel afterwards? Remember the quote from Democritus once again, "If you throw moderation to the wind, even the greatest pleasures can bring you pain." You should learn to eat in moderation, control your portions and fill what's left with water.

Screening and Check-ups

We take our cars, which are not as important as our bodies, for periodic servicing or annual checks, so why shouldn't we get checked up with regards to our health as well? It is a no-brainer that we need to get our bodies checked from time to time. Some people are lucky to be living in countries that have screening programs for both men and women at certain ages for some diseases such as cancers, whereas for many people living in some other countries you have to be proactive. Regardless of which side of the divide you live on, decide to go to your health professionals at specified intervals, say yearly, to get things like your blood tests, blood pressure, blood, bowels, breasts and cervix or prostate checked out. By doing this, you can detect things at the pre-disease stage when, with the help of your health professional, you might be able to prevent some of these diseases from becoming full-blown - or reduce their effect on your quality of life before they cause complications. You are ultimately responsible for getting this done, not your health professional or your health system. Be pro-active rather than reactive. Remember you have only one body, if you look after it, it will take you far.

Learning from Practical Examples

Meet the Centenarians of Ogimi

The Japanese village of Ogimi, located in the northern part of Okinawa, Japan, has the world's longest-lived people. Despite being a small village of just about 3000 people, they have over 14 centenarians and over 158 people aged above 90. For this reason, it is commonly called the 'Little Village of Longevity.' What is fascinating about this village is not the fact that people merely live longer, which we might have also noted in some Western societies where medical care is at its best, but rather that the elderly are healthy almost until the last days of their lives.

Up till the 1970s, there was no official hospital on this island and yet there were no reports of diseases such as diabetes or cardiovascular diseases.[30] Studies show that the inhabitants of this island are 80% less likely to die from a stroke, cancer or cardiovascular disease compared to the Western population. What's also interesting is that, although they have the largest proportion of centenarians in the world, more than three times the number found anywhere else in the world, diseases commonly labelled as diseases of old age, such as Alzheimer's, are rarely seen in their population.

Engraved on a famous stone monument in the centre of Ogimi is the following inscription: *"At 80 years old, I am still a child. When heaven calls for you at 90, say, "Go away and come back when I am 100. Let us keep going strong as we get older, and not depend too much on our children in old age."*[31] This village has sparked a lot of interest among scientists and researchers, who have attempted to study the inhabitants to find out why they live so long and have healthy lives. A couple of researchers have attempted to attribute this to their genes. However, a growing influx of Western culture, which is being adopted by the younger generation of the community, leading to the increasing incidence of obesity, cardiovascular diseases and premature death in this subgroup, disproves this. Besides, people who have emigrated from the village or the larger island of Okinawa have also had similar cardiovascular risk profiles to the residents of the new areas they have migrated to.

It is therefore important to learn from the lifestyle of the centenarians of Ogimi. They attribute their longevity to an active lifestyle, low-calorie healthy diets and an incredibly social community life. In the lovely subtropical climate of Ogimi, the residents are easily seen being active and working in the fields up till their latter years. A significant number of them exercise and walk regularly, and also take short periodic naps. Retirement is almost unheard of in this village, with many of the elderly people still working as dancers, tofu producers and association presidents.

The residents of Ogimi eat what is available to them, which typically are fresh and raw foods, mostly vegetarian and fish-based with only a little amount of salt. They drink a lot of tea, which has a strong antioxidant effect and also commonly produce and drink *Shikuwasa* juice made from small lemons, which contain a lot of Vitamin C. Residents consume a daily average of 1,800-2,200 calories compared with residents of Western societies that consume 2,200-3,300calories and they have lower body mass indices.[32]

The last secret of the people of Ogimi lies in their emotional wellbeing. They live simple lives and keep stress at bay. A concept which is closely embraced by the members of this community is known as *Ikigai,* which refers to happiness in being busy. These centenarians find what they love and keep doing it for as long as their bodies keep carrying them. Community participation is high in this region as people sing and dance together, and even mourn together. As a way of life, the people of Ogimi have decided not to worry and move on. The centenarians simply forget to die because they love what they are doing.

The centenarians of Ogimi, therefore, embody the concepts this chapter is trying to teach us. The aim is not to live long miserable lives at the mercy of the care of others, but rather to live long, active, healthy and meaningful lives. We can do this only if we look after our physical and emotional health by being active, eating right and living in a state of happiness. Remember if you look after your body, it will look after you, too. Take care of the vessel!

Reflection and Action Steps

- How important is your health to you?

- On a scale of 1 to 10, how would you rate how you look after yourself? Is there space for improvement?

- When was the last time you did some exercise? Are there minor tweaks you can add to your life so that you are more active?

- Are there any toxic substances that you are exposed to that you know you need to reduce or stop altogether?

- What proportion of your diet is made up of fresh natural foods and what proportion is made up of processed meals?

- Do you always eat to be full? Have you considered substituting some of your meals with fruits, vegetables or even water?

- Do you get enough rest or sleep in a day? When was the last time you took a break from work/family routine?

- Do events or happenings around you get to you easily? Could stress be affecting your health?

- How do you feel physically when you are happy? Which activities or pastimes make you happy?

- Try out a new relaxing activity this week.

Chapter 10

Nurturing Meaningful Relationships

As professionals, we can't sail on our journey on earth alone. We need to interact with other people, whether they are family members, colleagues, business associates or clients. Valuable and meaningful relationships are essential if we want to enjoy our lives. Many of us just try at communication and relationships as they naturally come to us, but the truth is that we can improve with interaction skills which make us unique as professionals.

I work in a profession where the way we communicate with our clients (patients) can be the differentiating factor between a good physician and a bad one. While good communication is overly stressed and even tested in exams in the training or courses for many professions, we've all come across professionals whose poor communication has led to serious complaints or even loss of businesses. Good communication is therefore not something to merely talk about, but something that needs to be developed on a personal basis by everyone. Whatever profession you hold, being able to build and nurture meaningful relationships with those around us will make life a lot easier for us, as well as others.

This book is not intended to be a communication manual, but I would just like to highlight some small changes to our approach which, if implemented, can massively make us develop better relationships.

Be genuinely interested

There are so many things competing for our attention in today's world. It has become really easy to be superficial with things like news feeds and stories, such that everything in this world has become a 'swipe and pass' movement. Despite this radical shift in the world's thinking, we all still crave attention and significance. We don't feel satisfied with people taking a glance at what we are about and moving on; we want them to be truly interested. We want to express ourselves more, and people who allow us to do so are the people we hold dear the most. This is one of the main reasons why people disagree when they are not allowed to express themselves. People also want to know you want more for them than you want from them. In our professional lives, we can make a huge difference just by deciding to be truly interested in what others believe, what they are doing and why they do the things they do. This is not a call to uncomfortably pry into people's lives, but mainly just taking time out to ask simple questions can go a long way. Examples of such questions include:

- How are things going in your life?

- How do you spend most of your time?

- What are you working on currently?

- What plans do you have for the weekend?

- Any interesting thing going on in your life?

- Are you happy?

These questions seem commonplace, but what they do is knock on the door of the other person's life, signifying that you are interested in who they are and what they are about. I have tried this approach at the different places I have worked, and it has made a huge boost in my relationship with the people I have come across - and I have earned greater love and respect from people because of it. A step further from being a good listener is also letting people know that you are available to help if they need you. I believe this is a gift, one of reassurance that the other party will remember for a long time.

Be a good listener

Closely linked with being genuinely interested is being a good listener. To start, there is no point in showing interest in people's lives if you are not ready to listen to what they have to say, as this might cause more harm than good. You might say what is the big deal in listening to people, isn't it just a matter of letting the sound filter through your ears? No, it isn't! Good listening is an active process, not a passive one. It involves taking actions in response to the message that is being passed across by the person you are dealing with. These actions vary depending on the individuals communicating, but could include things such as nodding of the head, answering with an intermittent Uhm-Uhm, doing some particular tasks, or whatever is required during the conversation. However, the true test of active listening is what happens after the conversation; how you respond to the individual some days after, how much of what was said you can remember, and how much of a change you have affected based on what you were told.

The same applies to organisations that have departments for responding to complaints or suggestions. The true proof that you are listening comes from the actions you take, or changes you make, based on what your customers or clients are telling you. Everyone wants to be listened to, and taking action based on what they have told you makes them feel even more special.

Take care of the small details

It's usually the small things in life that matter. As one of the famous artistes Usher Raymond rightly said in his song *Simple Things*, it's these simple things in life that we forget. For some of us, when we were younger, we might have visited friends' houses that were in states less than ideal. By spending time at this friend's house, despite its state, you probably discovered new things about your friend that you never could have known from a distance, and this strengthened your relationship. Similarly, we all live imperfect lives, and it is in picking up the small inconspicuous things in people's lives and positively highlighting them that shows that you are truly interested in them, and makes them feel special. This goes beyond titles, positions at work, achievements, and material possessions like houses, cars, etc., which are the obvious things everyone sees. The small, usually forgotten things are things like someone's name or its right pronunciation, the new hairstyle, how beautiful a smile is, appreciation for doing what they do, remembering and celebrating a birthday or anniversary, the importance of a hug, or just simply holding hands, or providing encouragement for someone you recognise is going through a painful or difficult time. Always look for the opportunities to find small similarities with other people that can connect you. It is those people who can recognise the importance of small things such as these, and capitalise on them, that go on to develop the best relationships with other people.

Show love and empathy

Love makes the world go round. I believe the reason for this is because when you emit love, like a boomerang, it goes around the world and comes back to you. To be loved, you have to love - there is no shortcut to this. I am not talking about romantic love at this point, although the same applies to romantic love. The easiest way to show love is to treat others how you would want to be treated, and you can always use this to assess how much you are showing love to others. If you would have wanted to be given another chance, giving other people another chance is the expression of love. If you would have loved to have a meal, giving another a meal is an expression of love. If you would have loved a new outfit, giving a new outfit out would be an expression of love.

Genuine love is the basis for empathy. Empathy is the expression of what you would have felt if you were in the other person's shoes. If someone is talking about how he painfully lost a loved one, and you are on the other end laughing, you will agree with me that you are not empathetic. The ultimate proof that you have good and healthy relationships is how much people love you, and how much extra they are willing to do for you. This makes a whole lot of difference in your family life, career, finances, and even your emotions. The only way to get more of this is to give more love. Remember, as Maya Angelou said, people might forget what you said, but they will not forget how you made them feel.

Join Networks

You must develop successful relationships with those within your immediate sphere of influence. If you, however, want to advance your growth as a professional, it is advisable to join networks. A network is a group of people who are united by a common interest and meet at specified intervals. Networks don't only provide support for your professional career or personal interests, but also open your mind to fresh ideas, knowledge or perspectives. Network or club meetings are also places to improve on your confidence or interpersonal skills, and can provide long and meaningful relationships. Most successful people belong to one or more networks that have presented them with opportunities to become who they are today.

Learning from Practical Examples

Meet Oprah Winfrey (1954–)

Oprah Winfrey was born in Mississippi to Vernita Lee and Vernon Winfrey on an isolated farm in Mississippi in 1954. Her father was a coal miner in Tennessee and her mum a housemaid. Her parents separated soon after her birth and left her in the care of her grandmother. Although Oprah was born into poverty, and despite being a victim of sexual abuse several times in her childhood, she has managed to attain a level of fame and success by her own efforts in an unprecedented fashion. Today, she ranks as one of the most powerful and influential women in the world.

Winfrey had always dreamed of being famous since childhood, as she used to play-act in front of the farm animals as a kid. She also gave speeches at her church, social gatherings and speaking contests. One such speaking engagements earned her a scholarship to Tennessee State University. She started a career in broadcasting and journalism, but her real rise to fame was when she moved to Chicago and took over the role as anchor of a morning talk show called A.M. Chicago. The show had previously been ranked last in several ratings, but once Oprah added her personal touch and changed the emphasis of the show, its ratings and popularity increased. It eventually became known as The Oprah Winfrey Show in 1985.[33] Winfrey has capitalised on the success of her talk show which ran for 25 years, and turned it to a successful media and business empire. She launched her own cable channel OWN in 2011, is also a brand ambassador, and owns a stake in Weight Watchers. According to Forbes, the profits after reinvestment from her show add up to an estimated $2 billion.[34]

Although Oprah attests she has been talking and listening for a living for many years, the success of Oprah's talk show can probably be attributed to one major factor - her extra-ordinary interpersonal skills.

Having conversed with everyone from all walks of life, from homemakers and schoolteachers to leaders and politicians, she believes that great communication begins with connection.

Oprah's empathy is exceptional, as she always makes her guests and audience accept that she was one of them. Oprah has also on several occasions discussed her childhood, including poverty, neglect, drug problems, sexual abuse and teenage pregnancy. Her remarkable character of being open, vulnerable and compassionate always makes her listeners feel a deep and personal connection with her. Her unique ability to remain incredibly human and humble regardless of who she is talking to is what many regard as the true reason for her success.

She is also an excellent storyteller, as she has shown several times on her shows and at several public events. Another unique asset of hers is the use of body language and other non-verbal communication cues. Before Oprah, there was hardly any other talk show host whose emotional expressions synchronised with those of her guests as well as she has done. She has been known to cry, laugh, frown and even gasp in response to what her guest is talking about during her shows.

Oprah believes communication is like a dance in which the two parties are in a state of flow. Just one misstep can lead to disruption in this state of flow and lead to confusion. She believes this, however, is the perfect opportunity to find out what the other party truly wants. Listening closely and letting the other party know that you have truly heard, and value their thoughts or opinions, is probably the most important element in establishing your connection.[35]

Reflection and Action Steps

- What is the status of your relationships with the people around you?

- Do you focus more on talking or listening in your conversations with people?

- When was the last time someone opened up to you on intimate issues bothering them? How did you respond?

- Do you know the names of your colleagues, co-workers or clients?

- Are you part of a professional club or network? Are you an active member of this network?

- When was the last time someone showed some appreciation for the love you demonstrated?

- Write out an aspect of your communication that you would like to improve. Start working on it today.

Chapter 11

The Paradox of Giving

Some things in life appear counter-intuitive or difficult to explain, but this does not mean they are untrue. Whichever theory you believe about how this universe was created, you will know for certain that the universe always seems to find a balance. Whether you think it is God, or maybe you believe it is all explained by science, you will agree that there is an order, an unwritten set of laws to almost everything that happens on our planet. Look at how the day is always followed by the night, how the seasons come and go, how whatever goes up has to come down and you will agree that certain things are not only predictable, but certain.

What has all of this got to do with being successful at what you do? If you have read this book thus far, you will have come across some tools or techniques to improve your value, physical health, legacy, net-worth or your productivity. But there is one last one - the most important one; I decided to save the best for last. You do not need to be a psychic to know that I am about to talk about 'Giving.' This is another of the universal laws that cannot be broken.

The universe always finds a way to bless or replenish those who give. Look around you. Although you may find it hard to agree initially, on a closer look you will realize that the most successful, wealthiest, happiest and most fulfilled of people have a track record of giving far beyond what seems reasonable. You might want to think of that odd exception of a stingy rich fellow which you have come across somewhere in your lifetime, and argue that this law is not true, but I can tell you if indeed this individual is not a giver and is yet wealthy, it is either not genuine wealth or it is not destined to last. I can name several examples: people like Bill Gates and Warren Buffet, who pledged a huge chunk of their wealth towards causes such as fighting hunger, Malaria and HIV. These people should no longer be among the wealthiest people in the world anymore since they have given out such a huge chunk of their wealth, yet they remain there at the top. Have you stopped to ask yourself why? It is because the universe gives back to those who give; it is an invisible and irrefutable law.

Giving back not only ensures that we are in a state of steady supply; it also improves our physical and mental health. Some studies have shown that giving has a positive effect on our health and happiness. I may not be able to fully answer how this happens, but check out these facts. Some scientists believe giving helps our brain to release endorphins, similar to what happens when people take opioids. These endorphins help to blunt pain, and also produce a state of euphoria that is commonly referred to as 'high' on the streets. I do not know about you, but if giving can help take away pain and make me feel happy without side effects, then I am happily subscribing to it. Several other studies have shown that elderly people who volunteered or offered help to friends or neighbours were less likely to die over a five-year period, compared to those who didn't, or those who were on the receiving end.[36]

Many people think of giving as only about money but, most times, it is not about money at all. It is about giving your time, a listening ear, a warm hug or shoulder to lean on, a voice for the less privileged in our societies, a meal to the hungry. I came across an article by Joshua Zuchter online, and in this article he listed some random acts of kindness; they include the following: paying ahead for the order of the person in line behind you at your local coffee shop, kissing your partner out of nowhere in mid-sentence while he/she is talking, hugging your son or daughter for no specific reason whatsoever, telling one of your colleagues how great he or she looks in that colour or style, bringing your neighbour's recycling bins up to their garage doors, sending an email of gratitude to a friend with whom you haven't spoken in a while, finding out your colleagues' birth dates and surprising them with e-cards on their special days, or genuinely smiling at someone you know or even don't know.[37] Most of these random acts do not require any money at all, but can help to make someone's day. Why not be that person?

I think another universal principle related to giving is this - "Not everything that is yours is for the keeping." If you consume or keep it all, it grows bitter, sour or painful. Those who know a bit about the Bible would resonate with the story of Adam and Eve, who had all of the luxurious Garden of Eden to themselves, to consume at will, all except the fruit from just one tree called 'The Tree of

Knowledge of Good and Evil.' As a similar illustration, think of most of the fruits that we consume today, all of which except the seed is meant to be consumed. The seed is either painfully difficult to consume, or bitter, and could sometimes even be dangerous. Not only do you feel the pain or displeasure from consuming your seed, instead of giving it out or sowing it, but you also are at a disadvantage because you have missed the opportunity to reap from it in the future. Note this, if you do not sow anything, you do not stand a chance of reaping anything.

The water bodies which we see around us also serve as practical examples of this concept. The bodies of water which keep to themselves, not giving to any tributary, are usually the stale stagnant ones; however, those that are constantly giving as they receive are the freshest sources of water, those we like to drink from and relax in. Real-life examples of this illustration can be drawn from the Dead Sea and the Sea of Galilee in Israel. Both of them receive from the River Jordan but the Dead Sea retains all and gives to none, and therefore remains 'dead.' The Sea of Galilee is sparkling, fresh and full of life because, instead of retaining it all, it gives all of its water to others. Giving and sharing gives us joy and revives us. Imagine what you do when your child was born or you passed an exam; the first thing you would want to do is to share such good news and pass it on. This is simply because it makes us feel better in ourselves. Similarly, when you go out of your way to help those who are desperately in need in the society, and you notice the impact this makes in their lives, you feel a deep sense of fulfilment that you can't find from doing any other activity. A lot of people are quoted as being successful, but if you check their lives they do not feel fulfilled. Many times, the missing link is in finding a cause greater than themselves. That missing link is giving.

What I am trying to infer from all of this is that giving is one of the unbreakable laws of the universe. Tony Robbins puts it this way; "The secret to living is giving." From today, find a way to give beyond yourself. It could be through tithing and offerings to your local church, it could be giving to charity, teaching for free at an underprivileged school, donating clothes to the homeless, paying for healthcare for the sick, helping with the distribution of aid to areas struck by natural disasters, or whatever it is you can think of. The list is endless; just start from somewhere today. All your possessions or earnings are not meant to be kept to yourself. Life always reverts to an equilibrium, more is given to those who give, so they can give more. Fortunately, those who withhold get less, so they have less to withhold.

As Jesus said, "He that is faithful in that which is least is also faithful in that which is much."

Learning from Practical Examples

Meet Chuck Feeney (1931-)

Charles Francis "Chuck" Feeney is an Irish-American who was born in 1931. He grew up in an blue-collar community in New Jersey during the age of the Great Depression. He schooled at St. Mary of the Assumption High School, to which he has credited his charitable spirit. He worked for the US Air Force during the Korean War and later went on to study at Cornell School of Hotel Administration. His business career started when he got involved in selling tax-free liquor to US naval sailors.

He eventually partnered with some other colleagues and formed the Duty-Free Shoppers (DFS) Group, which gave rise to duty-Free shopping as we know it today. The DFS group expanded to selling tobacco, perfumes, cars and liquor to servicemen and tourists, and by 1964 had over 200 employees in 27 countries. The DFS group made a fortune when the Japanese economy boomed and travel restrictions were lifted for its citizens, allowing many of them to travel and spend their savings from over the years. Over the next decade, Chuck received $334 million in dividends, which he reinvested into hotels, clothing lines and tech startups.[38]

He secretly formed his foundation, The Atlantic Philanthropies in 1982 and transferred his entire stake in DFS, then worth $500 million, to his foundation. He had been secretly giving away his wealth through this foundation to various causes, including education, science, healthcare, ageing and civil rights and in several countries, including, the U.S., Ireland, Vietnam and

Australia. Chuck likes to throw big money at big problems. For example, he has donated around $1 billion to education in Ireland, up to another $1 billion to Cornell University, his Alma Mata, and over $350 million to strengthen the healthcare system in Vietnam. He also signed up to the Giving Pledge. All of this he has managed to do without blowing his own horn. It was not until 1996, when some of the stakes in DFS were sold to Louis Vuitton Moet Hennessy (LVMH) that it became apparent to the public that Feeney had transferred all of his wealth to his philanthropic foundation.

Throughout his life, Chuck Feeney has given away more than $8 billion and there is hardly any other person at his wealth level who has completely given away their wealth while still living. He intends to teach a new way of philanthropy to that which many other philanthropists practice – giving away your wealth while you are still living, rather than after you die. When asked where he gets his happiness from, Chuck remarked, "I am happy when what I am doing is helping people, and unhappy when what I am doing isn't helping people."

Today, Chuck still looks for ways to invest, with the intention of giving it all away through his foundation. Bill Gates once said about him, "Chuck Feeney is a remarkable role model and the ultimate example of giving while living."[38]

Reflection and Action Steps

- What are your thoughts or feelings about your possessions? Do you believe in your sole ownership?

- Do you find it hard to let go of something that belongs to you?

- Have you ever received a gift from someone when you least expected it? How did this make you feel?

- How can you offer your professional knowledge or service for free to help the course of humanity?

- When was the last time you demonstrated a random act of kindness? Try a random act of kindness this week and note how it made you and the other party feel.

- Commit to a regular giving plan e.g. to charities, orphanages, religious organisations.

Conclusion

Life on Your Terms

At the end of the day, what matters the most to you? The biggest regret of most people on their deathbeds is usually not the fact they did not make enough money, or that they did not live to a hundred; many times it is that they didn't live a life of full expression – they didn't get to show their loved ones how much they cared, they didn't start that business or pursue that career, they didn't reconcile that broken relationship, they didn't explore the world, they didn't give enough to those who needed it the most.

This book has been written for all professionals in all spheres of life. I hope I have pointed you in the direction of new concepts and mindsets, that will help you move towards living a 'successful' life, regardless of your path, journey or goals. However, here is the big question - why in the world should you aim to be successful? This question is important, as very many people do not consider it until they hit the peak they used to dream of as success, and ultimately find emptiness there. Every so often, we hear of another celebrity who has had a breakdown or committed suicide, despite the massive fame and success they have attained. Success is not an end-point; it is only a means for you to reach out for your ultimate fulfilment.

Go to some of the most deprived places in the world, where people live practically from hand to mouth, and you will be amazed to find the number of people who are happy with their lives, and literally could not wish for anything more. In contrast, even in the most developed of societies, you can readily find wealthy people living in abundance who are yet miserable, angry, depressed or even suicidal. The reason for this is because we have different definitions of what success truly means - it is in living a fulfilled life, having lived life on your terms regardless of your means. I particularly like the way Tony Robbins puts it – "Success without fulfilment is the ultimate failure!"

A practical step for all of us would be to take a break from the hustle and bustle of life and reflect on what we would want to be known for, what we think would bring us fulfilment if achieved, even if death calls at an early age. It might be one single thing, which some people call their 'life purpose,' or it could be a list of things - like your bucket list. For example, I believe I find fulfilment in spending my time and energy on things that I enjoy doing, and not on what others expect from me. I also hold my relationships dear as I believe I should never be too busy for the people that matter to me. I also derive joy from being able to give back to those who have needs but cannot help themselves, and that is why I give to causes such as those interested in children's education.

Each person will have their life purpose(s), and it is important to recognise them and work towards them. What is it that makes you

128

tick? Is it spending quality time with your family, or building a legacy for the generation after you? Is it career fulfilment? Is it having enough money to go on unlimited cruises round the world? Is it giving back to your community? Remember, only you can define what is most important to you. Writing or storing this somewhere you can readily access it is a helpful step, as it not only serves as a reminder when your mind goes into a blur, but it also serves as a motivator and compass as you navigate through life's stormy waters.

Success will eventually come, especially if you do all the right things and are diligent. True happiness, however, will only come when your soul finds what it is destined and has always longed for. If you forget all that I have written in this book, but remember this last paragraph, then my mission is accomplished. I sincerely hope you find true happiness and fulfilment in your personal and professional lives.

About Teach For Nigeria

According to UNESCO in 2013, Nigeria was ranked as the country with the highest number of out-of-school children in the world, approximately 10.5 million. The statistics reflect a broken system that makes it difficult for Nigerian children to receive an education, consequently making it impossible for them to fully reach their potential.[39]

Established in 2017, Teach for Nigeria (part of the Teach for All Network) exists to change this narrative. Their vision is that, one day, every Nigerian child will have the opportunity to attain an excellent education.

Teach For Nigeria recruits Nigeria's most promising future leaders from varied disciplines to teach in Nigeria's underserved schools in low-income communities, through a highly selective, two-year Fellowship. After the Fellowship, alumni of Teach for Nigeria build on their classroom teaching experience to drive long-term systemic changes in the educational sector in Nigeria as they progress into leadership roles in their varied professions.

I believe I would not be where I am, or have had the opportunities I have had today, if not for the education I had in childhood; I believe every child deserves this same access to quality education.

For this reason, I will be donating part of the proceeds from sales of this book to the Teach for Nigeria foundation to empower children who otherwise might not have had access to quality education.

For more information about this organisation, or to find out how you can give towards this cause, you can visit their website at www.teachfornigeria.org

Tunde Kukoyi

Bibliography

1. Gladwell, Malcolm. *Outliers: The Story Of Success.* New York: Back Bay Books, 2011. Print.

2. The Holy Bible, English Standard Version. ESV® Text Edition: 2016 www.biblegateway.com

3. Clason, George S. 1874 – 1957. *The Richest Man in Babylon.* New York, N.Y.: Penguin, 1957. Print.

4. Trump, Donald; Kiyosaki, Robert (2006), *Why We Want You to Be Rich: Two Men, One Message*, Rich Press, ISBN 978-1933914022

5. Grace Elizabeth Groner Foundation. "Grace's story", 8 May 2020, https://www.gronerfoundation.com/grace-s-story

6. Keilman, John (March 6, 2010). "A hidden millionaire's college gift - Grace Groner leaves $7 million to her Illinois alma mater. Few friends knew of her wealth." Lake Forest, Illinois: Los Angeles Times. 8 March 2020

7. "Bill Gates" *Entrepreneur*, 8 October 2008, www.entrepreneur.com/article/197526. 10 May 2020

8. "Bill Gates" *Biography.com*, A&E Networks Television, 8 April 2020, www.biography.com/business-figure/bill-gates, 10 May 2020

9. Gates, Bill. "What I Learned from Warren Buffett", *Harvard Business Review*, 28 May 2015, hbr.org/1996/01/what-i-learned-from-warren-buffett. 10 May 2020

10. Fitzgerald, Maggie. "More than 60% of Bill Gates' wealth is invested in stocks." 17 September 2019, https://www.cnbc.com/2019/09/17/bill-gates-gave-away-35-billion-this-year-but-net-worth-didnt-drop.html. Accessed 10 May 2020.

11. Kiyosaki, Robert T., and Sharon L. Lechter. *Rich Dad, Poor Dad: What the Rich Teach Their Kids About Money That the Poor and Middle Class Do Not!* Paradise Valley, Ariz: TechPress, 1998.

12. Hecht, Anna. "Shaq: 'I don't invest in companies just to try and get the big hit" 4 September 2019, https://www.cnbc.com/2019/09/04/shaq-i-dont-invest-in-companies-just-to-try-and-get-the-big-hit.html Accessed 11 May 2020.

13. Parker, Garett. "How Shaquille O'Neal Became a Successful Entrepreneur" (2016) Money Inc https://moneyinc.com/shaquille-oneal-entrepreneur/ Accessed 11 May 2020

14. Robbins, Anthony, and Peter Mallouk. *Unshakeable: Your Financial Freedom Playbook*, 2017. Print.

15. McBreen, Catherine S., and George H. Walper. *Get Rich, Stay Rich, Pass It On: The Wealth-Accumulation Secrets of America's Richest Families*. Portfolio, 2007.

16. Gerber, Michael E. *The e-Myth Revisited: Why Most Small Businesses Don't Work and What to Do About It*. Harper Business, 2011.

17. Berg, Madeline. "The Greatest Investor You've Never Heard Of: An Optometrist Who Beat The Odds To Become A Billionaire." *Forbes*, Forbes Magazine, 19 February 2019, www.forbes.com/sites/maddieberg/2019/02/19/the-greatest-investor-youve-never-heard-of-an-optometrist-who-beat-the-odds-to-become-a-billionaire/.

18. "Dr Herbert and Nicole Wertheim Family Foundation – Making Life On Earth Better." *Dr Herbert and Nicole Wertheim Family Foundation*, www.wertheim.org/.

19. Tepper, Taylor. "Many Americans Are Satisfied With Their Inadequate Emergency Savings." *Bankrate*, Bankrate.com, 12 April 2019, www.bankrate.com/banking/savings/financial-security-june-2018/.

20. Chapman, Ben. "Nearly Two-Thirds of UK Adults Don't Have a Will, Research Finds." *The Independent*,

Independent Digital News and Media, 9 January 2018,
www.independent.co.uk/news/business/news/nearly-two-
thirds-of-uk-adults-dont-have-a-will-research-finds-
a8148316.html.

21. "Warren Buffett" *Forbes*, Forbes Magazine,
www.forbes.com/profile/warren-buffett/ Accessed 15
May 2020.

22. Investopedia. "How Does Warren Buffett Plan to
Bequeath His Estate?" *Investopedia*, 31 January 2020,
www.investopedia.com/ask/answers/021615/who-does-
warren-buffett-plan-bequeath-his-estate.asp.

23. Insider, Business. "The Rags-to-Riches Life Story of
Alibaba Founder Jack Ma." 2 March 2017,
www.inc.com/business-insider/alibaba-jack-ma-life-
story.html.

24. Gregersen, Erik. "Jack Ma." *Encyclopædia Britannica*,
Encyclopædia Britannica, Inc., 6 Sept. 2019,
www.britannica.com/biography/Jack-Ma.

25. "Jack Ma." *Forbes*, Forbes Magazine,
www.forbes.com/profile/jack-ma/.

26. Elkins, Kathleen. "Richard Branson Wakes up at 5 A.M.
Every Morning-Here's His Daily Routine." *CNBC*,
CNBC, 30 November 2017,
www.cnbc.com/2017/04/11/richard-branson-wakes-up-
at-5-a-m-each-morning-heres-his-routine.html.

27. Cain, Aine. "A Day in the Life of Billionaire Richard Branson." *The Independent*, Independent Digital News and Media, 6 August 2017, www.independent.co.uk/lifestyle/a-day-in-the-life-of-billionaire-richard-branson-a7879266.html.

28. Cain, Aine. "A Day in the Life of Billionaire Richard Branson." *The Independent*, Independent Digital News and Media, 6 August 2017, www.independent.co.uk/lifestyle/a-day-in-the-life-of-billionaire-richard-branson-a7879266.html.

29. Parker, Clifton. "Embracing Stress Is More Important than Reducing Stress, Stanford Psychologist Says." *Stanford News*, 9 April 2016, news.stanford.edu/2015/05/07/stress-embrace-mcgonigal-050715/.

30. "The Village of Longevity" *The Story Institute*, www.thestoryinstitute.com/ogimi.

31. Readhead, Harry. "How to Live Forever*, According to a Japanese Longevity Chef." *Metro*, Metro.co.uk, 11 December 2019, metro.co.uk/2016/11/25/how-to-live-forever-according-to-a-japanese-longevity-chef-6281478/.

32. García Héctor, and Francesc Miralles. *Ikigai: the Japanese Secret to a Long and Happy Life*. Thorndike Press, 2018.

33. "Oprah Winfrey" *Biography.com*, A&E Networks
Television, 22 January 2020, www.biography.com/media-
figure/oprah-winfrey.

34. "Oprah Winfrey" *Forbes*, Forbes Magazine,
www.forbes.com/profile/oprah-winfrey/.

35. Winfrey, Oprah. "What Oprah Knows for Sure About
Communicating." *Oprah.com*,
www.oprah.com/spirit/what-oprah-knows-for-sure-
communication.

36. Suttie, Jill, and Jason Marsh. "5 Ways Giving Is Good for
You." *Greater Good*, 13 December 2010,
greatergood.berkeley.edu/article/item/5_ways_giving_is_
good_for_you

37. Zuchter, Joshua. "Random Acts of Kindness" *Joshua
Zuchter*, 22 April 2014, www.joshuazuchter.com/selfess-
random-acts-of-kindness/

38. Bertoni, Steven. "Chuck Feeney: The Billionaire Who Is
Trying To Go Broke." 22 July 2013,
www.forbes.com/sites/stevenbertoni/2012/09/18/chuc
k-feeney-the-billionaire-who-is-trying-to-go-broke/

39. "The Crisis" *Teach for Nigeria*, 14 May 2020,
teachfornigeria.org/the-crisis/.

About the Author

Babatunde "Tunde" Kukoyi is a medical doctor who grew up and trained professionally in Nigeria. He is currently working in the United Kingdom, where he is training to become a Cardiologist. His interests are reading, writing, personal growth and public speaking. He is also a proud member of Toastmasters International, a non-profit organisation that teaches public speaking and leadership skills through a worldwide network of clubs.

He is married to his lovely wife Amanda and together they have one son, Daramola. He believes that everyone has a reason for being here on this planet, and that the world can only become a better place if we all look beyond ourselves and contribute our quota to the good of humanity.

Feel free to connect via:

Website: www.tundekukoyi.com

Instagram: @drtundekukoyi

LinkedIn: Tunde Kukoyi

NOTES

NOTES